Selections from
HISTORY TODAY

General Editor
C. M. D. CROWDER

ENGLISH SOCIETY & GOVERNMENT IN THE FIFTEENTH CENTURY

A Selection of Articles from *History Today*
with an original introductory essay by

C. M. D. CROWDER

OLIVER & BOYD
EDINBURGH
LONDON

OLIVER AND BOYD LTD

Tweeddale Court
Edinburgh 1

39A Welbeck Street
London W 1

First published 1967

Printed in Great Britain by
T. and A. Constable Ltd
Edinburgh

PREFACE

In this collection I have chosen articles from the first fifteen volumes of *History Today* to illustrate some important aspects of society and government in late medieval England. The economic and social changes which are dealt with were not confined to the fifteenth century: but the political and cultural consequences of those changes became habitual and significant features of English life at this time. Professor Barraclough's article, standing first in the collection, does not deal in precise chronological limits like the others: but, as well as conveying the excitement which all historians derive from their primary sources, he indicates the dependence of the historian of the later Middle Ages on bureaucratic records preserved in widely separated archives. The opinions expressed in the introductory essay are based mainly on the works given in the Select Bibliography. In the nature of the case neither those authors, nor the authors of the articles in this collection, would necessarily endorse all the conclusions which have been drawn from their studies.

My task has been made much easier by the courtesy of the editors of *History Today*, who supplied issues containing the articles selected for reprinting. I would also like to thank the editorial department of the publishers of this book. They have corrected some statements in the text and in captions to the illustrations which it was not possible for me to verify personally. The imperfections are my own.

C. M. D. CROWDER

CONTENTS

C. M. D. Crowder

ENGLAND AT THE CLOSE
OF THE MIDDLE AGES

It has never been found easy to give a general impression of England and her people at the close of the medieval period. One of the contributors to this book has recently called the fourteenth and fifteenth centuries, roughly the period from St Louis to Luther, "one of the darker and more desolate spans of European history". The student of the late Middle Ages may grudge the description, but for the general reader it must probably be owned as true of England as of Europe. If the fifteenth century is identified at all, it is known by the apparently futile conflict of the Wars of the Roses. One reason why it is difficult to synthesise England's history at the end of the Middle Ages is that the nature of the sources changes in this period. On the one hand, the historian confronts a greater variety of material than at earlier dates; and Mr Kirby's essay shows what this may mean for the reconstruction of events on the basis of records. On the other hand, there is no chronicle tradition to provide a contemporary synthesis on which the modern historian can reconstruct his own inter-pretation. Another problem of the sources is illustrated by

Professor Barraclough's contribution. While England has never been isolated from Europe in historical times, by the fourteenth century the political and ecclesiastical structure of the Continent, as well as its economic and intellectual cohesion, was such that distant archives and foreign chronicles contain invaluable materials for the historian of England. Barraclough notes the surprises which he found in Koenigsberg. The impact of the heretical opinions of Wycliffe is seen in Bohemia as well as in England. We would have a much less complete view of the policies of the Yorkist dynasty without guidance from Burgundian and French chronicles; and some of the most vivid glimpses of the early Tudor court come from the archives of Milan and Venice.

A different factor has contributed to the difficulty which historians have found in giving a rounded, yet bold, portrait of England at the end of the Middle Ages. Every study must have limits, if it is to achieve its objective: but, if such definition is inescapable, it can be arbitrary and its effects impoverishing. It has been no help to the study of English history in this period that long tradition has sundered the Yorkist dynasty from the early Tudors. After a little cool consideration, nobody really believes that the rounding of the Cape of Good Hope or Columbus's voyages, the introduction of printing, or still less the Lancastrian victory at Bosworth, ushered England into the modern era. Every historian of this period, either as an undergraduate himself or setting a problem to his students, has probably proposed a comparison between the Yorkists, Edward and Richard, and the first Tudor, Henry VII, with the intention of correcting this simple dichotomy.

Yet most books still implicitly respect it. The two centuries from the start of the Hundred Years War to the English Reformation have no obvious unity. Yet they saw developments which little by little transformed English society and government as well as redistributing the country's wealth and modifying many accepted loyalties of her people. It is not easy to chart such an imprecise evolution; and it is no help having the full term of these developments cut off from their beginnings.

One further feature which has complicated a simple and summary interpretation of late medieval England should be mentioned. Was the country prosperous or did it suffer hardships at this time? It is not surprising that the answer comes differently from different social groups—and therein lies much of the ambiguity and apparent contradiction about late medieval England. Economic and social historians have consequently been unable to offer the general historian a prevailing pattern such as that which characterises English history from the Norman Conquest to the close of the thirteenth century. While this complexity and mobility of social fortunes provides the period with part of its interest, it has not promoted an accepted interpretation of the main themes of English development at this time.

What can be said, then, about England at the close of the Middle Ages?

Every age is prone to interpret the past in its own image, and there is an obvious danger of anachronism in doing this. Yet if one is to characterise the fifteenth century in a sentence, it is not wholly misleading to present it as the first step towards British social democracy. As in any historical generalisation, the detailed evidence must be subsumed in an intuitive grasp of the essential quality of a period; and for a period when the evidence is conflicting the subjective element in such a summary is bound to be great. So far as complex and contradictory evidence can legitimately be forced into a simple proposition, it would seem to resolve itself in this conclusion: that there was a measure of economic and social levelling. The gross national product was declining—at any rate until about the last quarter of the fifteenth century: but such prosperity as survived was shared more evenly among more hands. As Dr Warren points out in his discussion of the Peasants' Revolt, resistance to this distributive process was among the causes of the rising; and it may explain some of the peculiarities of that unparalleled movement upon which he remarks. This is far from saying that an egalitarian society was being created: only that the extremes of wealth and poverty were probably less by 1485 than they had been earlier at the death of Edward I, or were to be later, when Elizabeth I reigned. This wider distribution of the nation's wealth was not the result of any doctrinaire convictions, but of the play of economic and political forces. The nature of the former can be seen in Dr Warren's explanation of the background of the Peasants' Revolt. The profit to be made from actively farming great estates was being steadily overhauled by the cost of managing them (restocking, repairing, fees to officials) and of the political and social obligations attached to their possession. Many land-holders, though not all, were consequently disposed to let out more and more land at rent. Tenants were available among their more prosperous villeins, who saw their advantage in exchanging services for settled rent. They could also add profit to independence, since they did not have to carry the same overheads or obligations as the great lords, and were able to provide much of the necessary labour from their own families. Where new farms were carved straight from the lord's demesne, as was often the case, it was easier to manage them efficiently than when holdings were scattered over a number of strips. By these means the farming community was reinforced by the solid, independent virtues of a yeoman class, which directly in production and indirectly in payment of its rents contributed to the gradual accumulation of capital, which was available much later to back the early ventures leading to an industrial revolution. Commonplace as any reference to this middle range of rural society in England may be, its significance is not diminished for that reason. Sir John Fortescue, an Englishman who spent some years in exile in France in the middle of the fifteenth century, was struck by the oppression suffered by the French peasants. His observations were partisan: but at this time the difference between the holder of land and its cultivator was, indeed, being more sharply drawn in France and in the territories of the Empire.

In investigating life in the towns, we encounter the same difficulties; for here, too, any uniform interpretation must be derived from contradictory and local evidence. Despite gates and walls and curfews in many English cities, the division between town and countryside was not a sharp one. The yeoman also made his contribution here. The town was the market for his surplus, and in his turn, with other countrymen, he was a customer in its shops and stalls. The organisation of industry at this time further helped to blur the difference, since many processes in the developing cloth-trade could be carried on more profitably in villages and cottages than in towns where regulations were stricter, and where there was close supervision from competing crafts. It has recently been suggested, perhaps tendentiously, that clusters of clothing villages in the West Country, in East Anglia, and in Yorkshire, have as good a right to be considered towns, in every respect except their lack of corporate constitutional organisation, as the recognised boroughs and cities. Some of the cities fell on lean times in the fifteenth century. For instance, after a buoyant half-century, York and its chief port, Hull, slumped from about 1430 because of the diversion of raw wool to the clothing towns of Halifax, Leeds, Bradford, and Wakefield, whose produce was not yet a prominent export. Yet it is remarkable how business men manage to live well in bad times as in good; and York's fifteenth-century buildings and the vigour of its fraternities and guilds are sound evidence of the strength of her merchants' deposits, even if there was less going through their current accounts. Besides, if some places fell back, others grew more wealthy. Cities like Bristol and Salisbury, Norwich, Colchester, and King's Lynn prospered. So, too, did London, steadily increasing its share in the country's commerce and foreign trade just as it was increasing its share in its government, adding to its population, and incorporating surrounding villages and manors into its suburbs.

In the course of the re-alignment of urban prosperity total wealth declined by comparison with the buoyancy of

England's economy earlier in the Middle Ages: but, as in the countryside, it was spread more evenly among the merchant class. The Company of the Staple, which obtained an official monopoly of the export of wool by 1399, represented the victory of substantial merchants, acting as a consortium, over tearaway tycoons; and the competition which the Merchant Adventurers provided in the fifteenth century did not upset this balance. At the same time, native merchants succeeded in establishing themselves as the principal agents of England's trade without driving out foreigners. Italians continued to be familiar figures in southern England and the Midlands as brokers in the cloth-trade; and at intervals throughout the fifteenth century there was a trade war with the German Hanse as bitter as any later struggles with the Spanish or the Dutch. Thomas Betson (who died in 1486) is a representative and sympathetic figure of the English merchant with foreign interests. Member of the Staple, constantly on business in Calais, the Company's Continental bridgehead, his commercial links ran through London to his base in Oxfordshire. In business, and by marriage, he was closely attached there to an established landed family of local importance, and his letters surviving among their correspondence show him as the embodiment of bourgeois virtues: dependable, devoted, genial, and patient, the epitome of a class which was prosperous and homely.

Betson was a man whose horizon was bounded by his business and his home, a man who valued law and order, an ageless paragon of the civilian virtues. It may seem anomalous to suggest that he is a representative figure of

society earlier, and this has lent the late medieval arrangements the unfortunate label of "bastard feudalism". The retainder was in fact a very flexible instrument, and it had gained popularity over the grant of a feoff because it could be adapted to a wide variety of different relationships serving different purposes. It is most familiar as the pre-eminent means of raising forces for service in the war against France. The common form of such indentures was settled by the middle of the century, when the English adopted the strategy of long destructive marches on French territory. They laid down in considerable detail the obligations which both parties to the contract undertook and the distribution of the gains which they expected to make from booty and prisoners. They have been described with reason as profit-sharing schemes not wholly dissimilar to the prospectus of a modern commercial company. By the time of the Wars of the Roses, a civil war, the net profitability to be expected had almost disappeared, for the chance windfall could be so easily lost at the next turn of the political wheel: but the indentured contract and the system of retainders survived. This alone is an indication that it served more varied purposes than mounting a campaign in war. Ordinary indentures, as they appear in the rolls of the public records of the Crown, or in the registers of the great lords, provide that the retainer's service should be for peace and for war; and this peacetime service did not mean a virtual suspense of all useful activity until a local scuffle should call the retainer to arms. There were many ways in which he might be peaceably employed in his lord's interest, from keeping his hunting or his wines to the many positions of high responsibility, like steward, auditor, or receiver, which were necessary to the administration of the wide possessions controlled by the remaining magnates. A motley crowd of servants, tradesmen, gentry, and even clerks were as likely as military retainers to be in receipt of fees under indentured contracts.

Without denying that fifteenth-century England was dominated by a warlike aristocracy, it is important to emphasise that civilian needs provided a reason for the prevailing social organisation. The Wars of the Roses placed a premium on the leadership of the magnates and their principal followers, and the fortunes of battle were deadly only to these higher echelons of society. By the exercise of common prudence, the rest of the country, and even the great cities, were able to avoid serious loss, with the result that a generation of intermittent civil war did not check the returning prosperity of the country. The inroads which the bloody battles of the two dynastic factions made in the ranks of the high nobility underlined a fact which was manifest already: that they lacked the numbers and the wealth for the increasingly complicated tasks necessary to the administrative and economic well-being of the kingdom. Their capacity to represent their inferiors, the proportion of the nation's wealth of which they disposed, even their military contribution to the country's strength, steadily diminished. At rare intervals even the social authority of the aristocracy was challenged, by the eccentric views of a radical theologian like Wycliffe or by isolated explosions of proletarian discontent. These were important changes. That they did not immediately overthrow aristocratic domination of England was due, in part,

to the successful assimilation of upcoming rivals. In part
it was due to effective rearguard action. If the feudal
baronage had been seriously depleted by the late Middle
Ages, some families could trace their heredity to the
Norman Conquest, and the interval left them with little to
learn about tenacity. As the Crown had called on other
groups and interests to take a share in the formidable task
of governing a medieval state, these magnates had taken
advantage of constitutional growth to consolidate their
ranks by the parliamentary convention of peerage. Since
the fourteenth century, the King's leading subjects had
expected to receive an individual summons to attend the
yearly or twice-yearly deliberations with their ruler which
had been normal practice. Though the Crown was free to
issue writs or to withhold them, there was no wholesale
dislocation of the customary distribution.

As in former centuries, the land was still the foundation
of this aristocratic dominance. It was the resources of the
land which provided the revenues and fees on which
bastard feudalism reposed. Land was the key to political
position, and inevitably there was jealous competition for
it. How bitter the competition could be is shown in Mr
Blow's article about the Berkeleys: it also shows some of
the methods of preserving and gaining estates. The year
1470 was a time of disorder when there was more opportunity for brute force to be successful. At other times
purchase was not to be despised, though it was possible
only for small parcels, and the sovereign way to add acre
to acre was by inheritance and marriage. Casualties among
the menfolk in foreign and domestic war, and the natural
tendency of long-established families to fail of heirs, pro-

vided the opportunities. The incentive for the accumulation of lands came from the pressure on profit margins accompanying the economic recession of the fourteenth century. It was no easy task to maintain revenue in the face of the inescapable increase in wages and fees, and in the hazards in the game of political snakes and ladders which great nobles could not evade. Correct decisions about the swaying dynastic fortunes were essential. The penalty for a wrong choice was never obliteration, and legal ingenuity could be employed to neutralise parts of the inheritance: but, as well as involving the loss of marginal estates, mistaken decisions meant the loss of office and pensions under the Crown which were a useful buttress for declining revenues. Even when the tide of politics was favourable, many resources were employed to bolster the falling return on landed property. In addition to fees from someone of still greater rank, or lower if he had them in his gift, it was necessary to guard against the loss of collateral lands at the same time as pursuing additions to the inheritance through marriage to an heiress. That the lady was of noble or common birth was of little account if she was well endowed with either land or capital, and her person was indifferent. War, especially foreign war, was a source of profit to many, on account of the fees for military service and the spoils and ransoms which were brought home. For a generation or so in the earlier part of the fifteenth century, profits could be shown on the estates taken up in occupied France. War at home was less rewarding. Victorious contenders for the Crown rewarded their followers with escheated estates, but they could be lost as easily when fortunes changed.

Economic and political conditions like these fell a long way short of overthrowing the established ruling class in England: but they kept it in a sufficient state of uncertainty and mobility for other groups to assure their interests. The affinities that were permissible between merchant families and the landed aristocracy have been generally recognised. Other socially less exalted groups, of peasant stock, also profited by the pressures which they could bring to bear on landlords afflicted by the consequences of economic recession.

The instruments by which law and order were secured are unequally represented in the following articles. The source of both was the King, acting with his Council and with Parliament. For good government co-operation between all three was necessary, and between them and the local agents with executive authority. The monarch was the central figure at every level. Whether in parliamentary statute or council ordinance, it was his law that guaranteed order, enforced by his courts, and implemented by his officials, or by officials using his authority. The Council, in which policy was discussed, was the King's Council. The King's central place in government is emphasised in many illustrations. One shows Richard II holding the symbols of his authority. In this volume, another pictures him at Smithfield handling a crisis in which he, and he alone, could arbitrate. At the other extreme the King is made the arbiter of literary taste or of leisured distractions, and Caxton was not troubled by dedicating his books to "his dread, sovereign lord" regardless of dynastic changes and how they were accomplished. At the same time the King was powerless on his own. He needed the

consent of those who mattered; and who these were
differed from time to time. Fortescue had urged the
exclusion of "the greatest lords of the land" from the
King's Council because they were already too influential.
Yet it may be doubted whether it was in deference to his
views that Edward IV and the early Tudors relied more
heavily than their predecessors on councillors of common
birth and legal training. There had been men of this type
acting in an official capacity in the Council much earlier,
and their increased prominence in the late fifteenth century
reflects the increased need for their services.

The search for the essential co-operation between the
ruling institutions, for a period soon after the usurpation
of the Lancastrian dynasty, can be seen most clearly in Mr
Kirby's contribution. Controlling the largest inheritance
in the kingdom, leader of a successful *coup d'état*, Henry
IV had the support of a great many of those who mattered:
but his early years were years of economic hardship and
beset with political difficulties, and in 1406 he was still
seeking to establish his house as custodian of the country's
welfare. Hence his respect for the membership of the
Council sworn in the Parliament of that year. The King
was free to choose his councillors as he would: but the
magnates expected to have a voice there, and the representatives of the country in Parliament liked to know who
was responsible for advice given to the King. That these
matters were insisted upon openly and prescriptively is a
sign that Lancastrian policy was in difficulties. The situation was similar when Henry V left a son nine months old
as his heir. Despite its divisions, this minority council of
the 1420s gained substantial independence of royal and

parliamentary supervision, and it established a reputation as a grave and responsible body. Its influence and initiative has no earlier parallel. Nevertheless, once Henry VI was of an age when he could rule for himself, an ambitious cabal which saw its interest in promoting the young King's personal control, neutralised the Council's corporate influence without difficulty or irregularity. The change is epitomised by the increased activity of a hitherto obscure official, the King's secretary.

Throughout the later medieval period there was uncertainty about where sovereign authority reposed, and not only among those with a stake in English politics. Fortescue, a former Chief Justice of the King's Bench, proposed a theoretical foundation in the proposition that England was a *dominium politicum et regale*, that its government combined royal and representative forms through which monarch, and those subjects who counted, each had a part in the rights and responsibilities of government. Fortescue's theory was not elaborate, and it had no more influence than his practical recommendations: but it is interesting, since it reflects a professional lawyer's experience of the faults of government in the last years of the Lancastrians and the early years of the Yorkists.

The practice rather than the theory of government is what concerned most Englishmen at the time; and in this collection of articles there are representative glimpses of the ruler's tasks. Richard II, little more than a child and supported by his Council, many of whom were objects of the rebels' anger, had to surmount the sudden crisis of the Peasants' Revolt. Henry IV, an experienced commander and successful conspirator, similarly with the advice of his Council, sought to balance the security of his French territories, especially the burdensome enclave of Calais, against inadequate resources. The war with France, the diplomatic manœuvring in defence of rights which were never doubted, and the provision of the means to uphold those rights on the battlefield were constant pre-occupations of the rulers of England until the reign of Elizabeth, when Spain for a time took France's place as the national enemy. Equally prominent, and of greater domestic concern, was the continual search for patronage and place and influence. In the Crown's gift lay the pensions and positions of power, the privileges and sources of profit, which the landed ruling class required. Subjects, whose rank or position made these available to them, continually petitioned the Crown to use its patronage on their behalf. In theory, and usually in practice, the decision lay with the King, acting on whatever advice he chose to command. The King was the greatest landholder of all, and he was not immune from the economic pressures which harassed his leading subjects. Much of his attention was given to the management of his own lands and house-hold, and the Yorkists and Tudors experimented freely in this respect. The public records of England are full of the decisions of the Kings and their officials in these matters of public and semi-public policy.

What has been said earlier about the prevalence of violence and about the prominence of a military aristocracy whose wealth lay in its lands should not be forgotten: but the contemplation of these careful sequences of bureau-cratic records establishes the impression that civilian values advanced in England in the fifteenth century. Even when they mirror aristocratic violence, these records indicate the unremitting attempt to absorb and correct such social vices. Professor Barraclough's article indicates that this was not exclusive to, nor novel in, fifteenth-century England. This helps me to make the chief point of this introductory essay. Because of a combination of diverse circumstances and the growth of distinct institutions, Englishmen at this date had reached a point where respect for civil, mercantile, or what in general parlance pass as bourgeois values, had become significant. It is echoed in the repeated demands of their representatives for "good governance".

If the greater part of this introduction has been given to a review of society and government, it is in the belief that these are the two most decisive aspects of any historical period; and that the transformations in these spheres which took place in the fifteenth century laid the foundations for England's history until the middle of the nineteenth century. Ideas are also important, but only those that contribute to the prevailing theme of this sketch can be briefly mentioned. The breakdown of confidence in the Church, which can be seen in widespread anticlericalism, in suggestions for the expropriation of the Church's wealth, and, for a time, in outright heresy, had one beneficial effect, in that it put men to school under the lay conscience. Much instruction of this sort came from obscure men, often artisans, and was heterodox and crude, but not all. The guilds and confraternities which attached themselves to urban parish churches engendered fervent devotion, and yet, one suspects, were only loosely attached to the direction of their clergy. This lay influence may have contributed to the conservatism of the English Reformation; and there is no doubt that it was partly a consequence of the spread of literacy to laymen. The schools, which in increasing number provided the basis of this knowledge of letters, were the product of pious benefactors, seeking a practical object for their faith and believing that this would be to the glory of God and his Church. These endowments were not intentionally anti-clerical: but it was harder for the clergy to control them than earlier types of benefaction. The growth of printing, which in England is so closely linked with the name of Caxton, contributed to the same result. The output of the new presses was predominantly sound religion, but the in-spiration which individual readers might draw from it was unpredictable. There was to this extent a levelling-up of intellectual achievement. From the fifteenth century, England's culture was no longer the preserve of clerks. The new presence which was beginning to claim influence in society and government was articulate and on the way to being self-conscious. That enquiring laymen were beginning to obtain the product which they needed can be seen in the rudimentary business training which was offered in Oxford on the fringe of the normal academic courses. It does not do to exaggerate the impetus given by one group to a slow advance on a broad front; but the lawyers, with their separate institutions of learning in the Inns of Court, their experience in private and public administration, and their services in the King's courts, equipped this lay awakening with a professional core.

The Continental Renaissance made a smaller contribu-tion to this movement than might be expected, although

Dr Myers shows one aspect of its influence in his account of the growth of the legend of Richard III. The lay culture of England was a vernacular culture, and patronage of Latin letters was left to high-ranking clerics and a handful of idiosyncratic nobles. Yet, if Miss Stuart's article on Caxton shows the English court to have had little sympathy with the Renaissance at the end of the Middle Ages, it also shows that it was not uninterested in cultivating the civilian arts. Domestic architecture offers further evidence of the demilitarisation of society, even of aristocratic society, as the alterations to many castles show. Merchants moved out of plague-infested cities to asylum in the country; and the differences between the external panoply of aristocrat and alderman began to diminish. A spate of books of manners appeared to help the new arrivals over the more ostensible hurdles. In a word, England was being domesticated; and it was not much later that the impression took physical shape in the countryside with the enclosure of fields and parklands.

The most obvious feature of fifteenth-century England is its unsettlement. Between the death of Edward III in 1377 and the accession of Henry VIII in 1509, there were seven changes of dynasty. Throughout these years there was either active war with France or the danger of war. There were repeated calls to arms in one connexion or another, for defence against the national enemy, or to decide an internal crisis by force. Add to these upheavals continual piracy around the coasts and repeated local forays in pursuit of private interests, and the total impression is one of chronic instability. It was, however, the nature of medieval society that these alarms rarely called on the resources of the whole people at any one time, and this book contains much which hints that more constructive forces were at work in late medieval England. The distinctions between social groups were being slowly bridged; despite difficulties, capital resources were being accumulated; government was being steadily pursued in a routine of order and co-operation. In an age when the authority of a narrow aristocracy was so prominent, there is no danger of exaggerating the advance of egalitarian forces: but by 1500 England was a more domesticated country than it had been before. It may have been less glorious, but it was more civilised and more comfortable. The contradictions do not make the fifteenth century easy to comprehend, yet they establish its importance in England's growth and its abiding interest.

G. Barraclough

THE HISTORIAN AND HIS ARCHIVES[1]

Archives are not history: but the historian who fails periodically to refresh himself in the fresh stream of original records soon ceases to be an historian. It is, of course, true that records do not, as so often alleged, "speak for themselves". No series of records, however complete, gives us more than a hint of past actuality; even the vast documentation now available for the history of international relations in the years 1933-9 requires a trained imagination, both to link it together in consistent order, and still more to relate it to all those underlying factors—assumptions, human failings, prejudices, beliefs, ingrained habits—which go unrecorded and yet colour every recorded statement. The undertones, the overtones, the pattern into which events seem to fall: all these it is the historian's business to bring out. But the records them-selves—not necessarily, of course, only the written records—are fundamental; and the farther he gets away from the records, the more likely he is to be beguiled by theories and reconstructions of his own making.

[1] [Copyright © G. Barraclough. Originally published in *History Today*, IV (1954), pp. 412-20.]

That records are "dry-as-dust" is a curious popular misapprehension. More often it is historical theory that is arid, precisely because it lacks that human touch which may suddenly transform the austere membranes of a Pipe Roll. It was by reading the thousands of twelfth-century charters which still exist in originals and in copies in the British Museum, with their crisp veracious detail, that Sir Frank Stenton and others broke through the barrier of smooth, unconvincing generalisations and gave us at last a living picture of the medieval English village. A score of similar examples could be cited, of the revivifying effect that immediate contact with records has exercised upon historical writing. An older generation of historians saw Henry III through the eyes of the monkish chronicler, Matthew Paris, and painted a stock picture of the "devout king", weakly yielding to his foreign relatives and the Pope, and more interested in lavish building than in politics and statecraft. The actual records have helped us to revise this estimate and have shown us Henry and his fourteen-year-old bride, Eleanor of Provence, as living human beings. The *Liberate* Rolls contain only orders for payment from the treasury: but there Henry and his Queen come to life as we read of the provision he made for her—

> of the rose of Provence painted on the walls of the queen's chamber and the stars stencilled on a background of vert and azure; of the cherry trees planted in her garden and the trellised way to her *herbarium*; of the "house of fir" he had built for her, "running on six wheels . . . roofed with lead"; of the figure of Winter, "made the more like winter by its sad countenance and other miserable attitudes of

the body", that Edward the son of Odo, keeper of the works at Westminster, was directed to have painted over her fireplace. We read, too, of the clasps and nails of silver for the royal book of romances; of the money paid to the clerks of the Chapel Royal for singing "Christus vincat"; of the fifteen lasts of "the best and most exquisite herrings" that the sheriff of Norfolk had to buy from Yarmouth and the lampreys which his brother officer of Gloucester had to place in bread and jelly and send to Westminster; of the dates and figs, pressed grapes and ginger salmon pasties, and mulberry and raspberry-flavoured wine, that figure so strangely in the records of State.[2]

Far more effectively than we may be prepared to admit, our vision of history is shaped by the records with which we ourselves are most familiar. When Leopold von Ranke, working in Italian archives after 1828, discovered the despatches of the sixteenth-century Venetian envoys and the State papers in the family-muniments of the great Roman aristocracy, and when later he found at Frankfurt on Main the official reports of the proceedings of the German Diets in the same period, not merely had he accumulated material for such famous works as his *History of the Popes* and *Germany in the Age of Reformation*: he also gave a twist to the study of modern diplomatic history, from which it had scarcely begun to shake loose even a century later. Modern Europe, with its characteristic system of the Balance of Power, was born (he thought) from the political and diplomatic combinations and conflicts which began in 1494; and as he progressed,

[2] Arthur Bryant, *The Story of England*, Vol. I (*Makers of the Realm*), p. 337.

the history of the seventeenth and eighteenth centuries, of the English Revolution, and of Frederick the Great, was brought into the same pattern. The belief in the decisive importance of policy at "cabinet level", which still dominated most of the writing on the origins of the war of 1914-18, goes back in origin to Ranke's discovery of the despatches, diplomatic reports, and instructions and protocols, of sixteenth-century Italy. It is the same on many other levels. The decision of Sir Henry Maxwell Lyte, when he became Deputy Keeper of the Public Records in 1886, to publish the great series of Calendars of English Chancery Records, has left an indelible mark on the study of English medieval history. Had he started with the Exchequer, the whole direction of subsequent research might have been changed, and, instead of administrative history, which has loomed so large since the days of Tout, we should almost certainly have found scholars concentrating on finance, possibly with important results in the consideration of such problems as the origin of Parliament. Even more incalculable were the results of the far-sighted action of Pope Leo XIII, when in 1881 he threw open the Vatican Archives to scholars of all creeds and nations. The great series of papal registers, beginning in 1198, revolutionised our views of the late-medieval Church; and, although for modern history the Vatican Archives have still not been used to the extent they deserve, the publication of the reports of the Papal Nuncios has profoundly influenced our conceptions of the period from the Reformation to the Peace of Westphalia.

Archives are not, as so often thought, simply a quarry,

C—E.S.G.

from which the historian excavates his "source-materials". On the contrary, they are, as Professor Galbraith once wrote, "an aspect of history itself", the "actual physical survivals of their age". The twelfth-century charter in the glass case may remain a mere museum exhibit: but no one who has himself handled it—as clean very often as the day it was written, the bold black ink standing out on the chalked surface of the parchment—who has studied its terse businesslike phrases, turned over the seal and pondered the idiosyncrasies of spelling and writing and the names and qualities of the long list of witnesses— Normans and English, knights and priests, butlers and cooks—will easily escape the sense of direct contact with the past which no amount of fine writing by modern historians can convey. Records have the harsh quality and texture of contemporary life: they are the real thing, not the *réchauffé*. Even the field I see, as I turn and glance out of the window, the bleak pasture of Astmoor, running down to what was once the wild Mersey estuary, looks different now that I know it from the fourteenth-century court-rolls.

It is no easy thing to convey the sense of excitement and expectation felt by the historian when he goes for the first time to a new collection of archives, fills in a slip, and waits for the first box or bundle of records to be placed on the table before him. I remember it, travelling through the orchards of Normandy to the Departmental Archives of the Orne at Alençon: but it was equally vivid on the trundling morning train from Cambridge to Bury St Edmunds, when I paid my first visit to the West Suffolk Record Office. It is the sense of discovery, the recognition that, in a single small document, a phrase or sentence may await one that will alter one's appreciation of a whole slice of the past, a fact that refuses stubbornly to accord with preconceived ideas, or perhaps the last eagerly-sought piece that completes the jigsaw. Or maybe it is just the knowledge of unexpected possibilities —as when, searching in Paris for materials a century and more later in date, I accidentally stumbled on the documents, casting new light on thirteenth-century politics in England, which the English barons submitted to Louis of France in justification of their resistance to the monarchy at the height of their struggle with Henry III.

The historian rarely goes to the archives without some clear purpose in mind; he usually emerges, if his mind is still open and receptive, with something very different from, but probably no less illuminating than, what he had expected to unearth. Though all archives contain a mass of incidental documentation, rarely spread over less than eight centuries, most of them—and certainly all the great archives—have their own special flavour and a hard core that determines their character. Thus the hard core in the English county record offices are the records of the Justices of the Peace, who, from the time of the Reformation down to the Local Government Act of 1888, were the uncrowned kings of the county, even though in sheer quantity these records may be outnumbered by the deposited documents, brought in from farms and country-houses, solicitors' offices, and old-established businesses. In the same way, the hard core in the Public Record Office in London is formed by the rolls and records of the royal chancery. The very site of the Public Record Office in Chancery Lane, the road which the Templars had built to connect their old home in Holborn with the new Temple off Fleet Street, was made available in the thirteenth century to house the growing numbers of enrolments. It was originally a home for converted Jews, founded by Henry III in 1232, which became derelict when Edward I expelled the Jews from England in 1290. The Master of the Rolls, the present "keeper" of all the public records of England, was originally only the keeper of this house and of the records of the Chancery preserved in it; and it is only since 1838 that the records of other departments of government, formerly scattered all over London from the Tower to Westminster, have been brought together in Chancery Lane and placed under his custody. Down to 1862, the State Papers, which contain the most important documents of government from the time of Henry VIII, were kept in a separate Paper Office in St James's Park; and even today there are departments which prefer to retain their own records under their own control.

The historian, who goes to the archives, will be prepared for surprises and, no doubt, for disappointments. All archives have their limitations. Because of the old habit among statesmen of treating the state papers which passed through their hands as personal property, he may find matters of high policy in documents deposited in a local record office, such as the Strafford papers now in Sheffield. But, in general, he will not go to the county record offices for the acts of central government. The historian of feudal England may rightly suspect that he will find relevant documents in the Archives of Normandy—at Caen,

Rouen, Evreux—and that he might, before they were destroyed in 1944, have found still more at St Lô. He would not go to Normandy, however, but to the *Archives Nationales* in Paris, if he were interested in the history of Anglo-French diplomatic relations. At the same time, he would be aware that Paris has nothing to offer for the history of French government before 1789 comparable to the continuous series of administrative records in London; and he would know that this was due not merely to accidents—like the fire of 1737, which destroyed practically all the early French financial records—but to the fact that the French monarchy never registered the acts of government with the systematic profusion of the English kings. If his work carried him to Germany, he would bear in mind the federal character of the German constitution from 1356 to 1871, and would not look in the archives of the Reich, which reach back only to 1867, for the records of earlier governmental activity and policy. Instead he would go to those of the constituent states, the "secret state archives" of Prussia, and of free cities such as Lübeck, which housed the archives of the Hanseatic League, a prime source of information on English foreign trade from the fourteenth century onwards. In Spain, there is a similar distinction. The records of Spanish policy in the "Golden Age", beginning with the emperor Charles V, are housed at Simancas: but the archives of the overseas dependencies, so important for the whole story of European expansion into the New World, are to be found in Seville. Before the union of Castile and Aragon in 1479, moreover, the Castilian records are sparse and relatively unimportant; and for the medieval period it is to the incomparable Archives of the Crown of Aragon in Barcelona that he would be most likely to turn.

But if all archives have their limits—if some tell us more of one period and less of another, while some remain essentially local—there are a few that may be said to be truly universal in character. The reason is that they reflect and represent the activities of a government or institution with universal interests, or perhaps with supra-national duties and functions. Such, it may be, were the archives of the Byzantine Empire at Constaninople, which provided in many ways the basic diplomatic forms for Western Europe. But these are no more, and the scanty records of Byzantine administration can now be haltingly reconstructed from the few "chrysobulls" scattered far and wide in the archives of their recipients[3]. A universal character might also be claimed for the Austrian archives, the *Haus-Hof- und Staatsarchiv* in Vienna, founded in 1749 by the empress Maria Theresa, covering the period when the Habsburgs were the rulers of a great multi-national European empire. But no historian should speak of archives that he has not studied personally; and among the archives of which I have personal experience, three stand out: the Vatican archives, those of the Teutonic Knights, and the Archives of the Crown of Aragon in Barcelona. If I try now to indicate something of the special flavour and character of each of these, it is because none is narrowly confined to the history of any particular land, and each contains material as important in its way for the English

---

[3] [Documents with a golden seal, issued by the Imperial Chancery at Constantinople prior to the overthrow of the Eastern Empire in 1453, are known as "chrysobulls".]

historian as documents he may find nearer home. We miss much if we read and study history on severely national lines; and the great archives which cut across national boundaries, and have something to say to historians of all countries, stand in a class of their own.

Most famous, without doubt, are the Vatican archives; for while the activity of secular rulers is territorially defined, that of the papal chancery extends over the whole of Christendom. And yet it is very easy for the novice to form a wrong impression of their character. First of all, the old registers of papal letters have nearly all disappeared; and it is only from the beginning of the pontificate of Innocent III in 1198 that we have a continuous series. Thus for the early history of the Papacy, of its influence over the Church and its share in the foundation of medieval society, we must search far and wide among the archives of Europe, among the muniments of episcopal sees and chapters and the records of dissolved monasteries—a laborious task requiring infinite time and patience, which was systematically taken in hand by the German scholar, Paul Kehr, in 1896, and is still proceeding. No other single undertaking of its kind has done more to deepen our understanding of the making of Europe: but in its execution the Vatican archives have played a very minor part. Nor, contrary to common belief, are the Vatican archives particularly notable for the number of famous documents they contain. The regular user soon learns to accustom himself to the idea that he will make no world-shaking discoveries, and that the peculiar value of the papal archives—and particularly of the papal registers—lies on another level. What they give us, above all else,

is the day-by-day story of papal activity, as it touched
every land, every city, every monastery, almost every
village of Christendom: an activity for which no detail
of Church regiment was too small, which found time,
even at periods when political questions demanded all the
Pope's energies, and when the Church itself seemed on the
brink of catastrophe, to counsel and guide individual
Christians among the heathen of Morocco or in the en-
campments of the Tartars. This mass of cumulative detail
illuminates the whole Christian horizon from Ireland to
the Gulf of Finland; and it is by adding detail to detail,
and building up a composite picture, that the worker in
the Vatican archives normally proceeds. As we read the
names of English villages, uncouthly written by Roman
clerks—Long Itchington, Little Oakley, Wetheringsett or
Wimborne, Ingoldsby Skipwith, Fillingham—in strange
juxtaposition with the place-names of Spain and Tuscany,
of Silesia and the snow-covered valleys of Norway, we
perceive that we are face to face with a world-power unique
in its day. As my own teacher, Rudolf von Heckel, once
wrote: "the world-wide dominion of the papacy resulted
to no greater degree from its leadership in the major affairs
of Church and State than from the endless number of
petty, constantly repeated, daily recurring transactions—
individually of small historical interest, but precisely
because of their separate insignificance all the more impressive as a body—through which the papal power
pentrated to the farthest parts of Christendom and made
itself felt in even the lowliest ranks of society".

The case of the Archives of the Crown of Aragon in
Barcelona is different. What is it that makes these the most

astounding medieval archives of the world? Here again we have archives that, interesting enough earlier, only come into the first rank during the thirteenth century; and in this case the external cause is obvious enough. It was the war of the Sicilian Vespers in 1282, that first drew Spain into the arena of Mediterranean politics, pitted Aragon against the combined might of France and the papacy, and started the Franco-Spanish rivalry for the control of Italy which, as is now almost universally recognised, marks the beginning of the modern system of diplomacy and international relations. The efforts of Aragon to defend itself brought it not only into relations with all the other countries threatened by French aggression—with Germany and with Edward I of England—but also with the great Islamic powers in Spain itself, in Morocco and in Egypt, on whose support or neutrality depended the control of the seas without which Sicily could not be held. This vast diplomatic activity makes the Aragonese archives unique in late thirteenth-century Europe. Embassies were sent out on a scale unprecedented; and their lively reports contain character-sketches and pen-portraits of personalities, like Pope Boniface VIII, incomparably veracious and vivid. They retail for us the *ipsissima verba* of kings and pontiffs, astoundingly modern in colour and tone, the secrets of diplomatic negotiations and all the rumours, reports, and news which passed from mouth to mouth in the courts of Europe.

And yet it needs more than this to account for the incomparable richness of the Barcelona archives. England and France were also deeply involved in the politics of the day: but, in this field, neither the Public Record Office

nor the *Archives Nationales* can vie with the Archives of
the Crown of Aragon. The explanation is that James II
(1291-1327), under whom the Aragonese archives
suddenly achieve an extraordinary profusion, was personally interested. It was said of him, in the papal court,
that he wrote more than all the other sovereigns of Europe
put together: he badgered his ambassadors pitilessly for
reports; he kept up a ceaseless correspondence with his
family, particularly with the daughters, whose marriages
played a great role in an age of dynastic alliances; and, for
the last twenty years and more of his life, every scrap of
paper was stored away, every letter registered. One
register alone, out of 339 volumes which still exist for
James's reign, contains over a hundred letters to and from
his daughter, Isabella, who had gone in 1314 at the age of
twelve to Vienna as the bride of duke Frederick of Austria.
Another, chosen at random, brings us, side by side, letters
to King Edward of England, the Sultan of Babylon,
Mahomet Abu Abdil Abenazar, King of Granada, the
overlord of Morocco, the emperor Andronicus II in Constantinople, and the Khan of the Mongols, as well as the
rulers of France, Naples, Portugal, Castile, and Germany.
And yet to suggest that the interest is primarily or mainly
diplomatic would certainly be wrong. No archives tell us
more of the lives of ladies of princely blood—and nothing
is more rare, until recent times, than authentic information
about the place of women in society; none, probably, more
of the religious cross-currents of the time. Books and
libraries, jewels, relics, alchemy, ship-building and trade,
crusades, the exploits in Greece of the famous Catalan
Company, the dawning Renaissance of the age of Petrarch

—these and a hundred other topics are illuminated by the documents in Barcelona. No single document is more curious, and few are better known, than the long factual account, attested by public notary, of the lady who, in 1319, claimed to have borne King James twin sons, when he was campaigning in Sicily in 1287—the King replied soberly that he had no recollection of it. Noticed by the King (she said) as he was riding past her house, she was taken the same evening—it was Ascension Day, Thursday, 15 May—by four gentlemen of his household to the king's chamber:

> and in the same chamber were three torches in three candlesticks, one throwing light on the head, another on the middle and the third on the foot of the bed ... and the bed was prepared with white unhemmed linen with a white pillow made from stuff of Bokhara, and with an edged coverlet; but what the edging was, she did not know. And the aforesaid Gerolda stayed a long time alone in the chamber. And afterwards the king came and entered the chamber and on seeing him the woman rose, for she had been sitting on the ground on a carpet. And immediately the king took her by the hand and questioned her. . . . And the lord king sat on the bed, which was low without legs, and made her sit on the same bed next to him at the lower end; and while they were thus sitting someone entered and, removing the hood, which he was wearing, knelt down and took off the king's shoes, which were scarlet with pointed toes, and undressed the king, leaving him in a vest of silk. And the servant went out, closing the door . . .
>
> And, to complete the record, the woman added that she was dressed in a gown of emerald green, and wore a turned-up headdress of the colour of gillyflowers ornamented with gold in the Calabrian fashion, and that her

belt was made of deerskin with silver, and had been her
father's. Her hair was done in the Latin style and was
pleasant enough to look at, on account of its sheen. Her
skin was pale, her complexion highly coloured, her face
animated and pleasing; she was then about 27 years old,
medium in height or even small. She said that the lord
king on the evening of Ascension Day made himself
known to her, saying: "Have no fear, for I am King
James!", and on the Friday morning he said to her:
"Rest assured that no harm will come to you!"

The Archives of Aragon retained their high quality and
universal interest for a century and more, and only declined
in profusion and importance as the kingdom itself lost its
place among the leading powers. The archives of the
Teutonic Knights, once housed at Koenigsberg in East
Prussia, but since 1944 at Goslar[4], acquire universal interest
at much the same period as the Aragonese archives begin
to decline. Here again, we have to do with an international
institution, one of the three great Orders of Chivalry
which arose out of the Crusades; and, although we mainly
remember the Teutonic Knights for their conquest and
settlement of heathen Prussia, during their first century
they had their headquarters at Acre in Palestine, and it was
only in 1309 that the seat of government was transferred to
Marienburg on the Vistula. But it is later, from about 1380,
when the Knights became more and more deeply involved
in a life-and-death struggle with the rising Slav nations
of the east—with Poland and Lithuania and later Muscovy
—that their archives become of primary importance. The
reason, once again, is their exposed position in the heart of

[4] They are reported to have been moved again since this article
was written.

Europe—and in a lesser degree the need to place on the market of the west the products of the newly colonised east—which forced them to maintain agents and embassies at all the courts of Europe, to collect reports of happenings from Scotland to Russia and Cyprus, to spend vast sums on espionage—a practice, also, of the Italian city states—and to negotiate treaties, defensive and offensive, with powers far and wide. The curious reader will be interested most of all by the reports of events on the confines of Europe and Asia: the references to Doulatbardi and Sedachmeth, emperors of the Tartars; the defeat of the Khan Chudandach in 1426; the prescription sent by an Indian doctor to the Grand Master in 1406; the progress of the Turks in south-east Europe, and the help it was rumoured they had received from Venice and the Poles. The serious student will pay particular attention to the despatches from the agent of the Order at the Papal Court which at some periods flow in month by month and almost week by week, and provide a vivid summary of the course of political events throughout the civilised world. But the English reader, intent only on English affairs, will also find here first-hand information which he would seek in vain elsewhere. Here, for instance, is an eye-witness account, still unpublished, of the Peasants' Revolt in 1381. Elsewhere we read how the English harvest of 1438 had failed, and the King was begging for the export of corn from Prussia. Attempts are made to enlist English archers for service with the knights against the Hussites of Bohemia. There are letters from James II and Queen Mary of Scotland on behalf of a Scottish merchant, James Lauder. Between the accession of Henry VI and the outbreak of the Wars of the Roses, a long series of "news-letters" brings us details of leading English personalities, the Beauforts and Humphrey, Duke of Gloucester, of the scene at court and the temper in the country; while other letters and documents bring us news of the Hundred Years War and English intervention on the Continent. Only after the Peace of Thorn in 1466, when the Order was forced to cede West Prussia with the leading cities of Marienburg, Danzig and Thorn to Poland, and the Grand Master himself became a vassal of the Polish king, does the stream of documentation dwindle and dry up. For the previous century, the archives of the Teutonic Knights are the richest of sources, many-sided and universal in interest.

I need add little in conclusion, for I have tried not to teach a lesson, but to draw a picture. To convey an accurate impression of the rich haul that awaits historians in archives such as those of the Crown of Aragon or of the Teutonic Knights would be an impossible task. Every selection falsifies; and, worse still, every selection narrows and sets limits to the richness of an almost inexhaustible field. But three things stand out. First, the suggestion that archives are "dry-as-dust" is totally misleading. Every document, of course, is not a gem of the first water; and the historian searching for a particular object may have to sort wearily through a pile of dross before he comes upon what he wants. But, even among the documents one turns over hurriedly, there are few that, if one but paused to enquire, have no story to tell. The second point is the direct appeal of the records, the direct insight into the past which they convey, and which no "secondary" writing, no matter how skilled, can quite recapture. It may be that they show us only a corner of the past: but that corner is revealed in the authentic colours, often crude but firm and unsmudged, and not as "a vanished picture of romance seen through Gothic windows". And, if our archives cannot show us the past as a whole, it is an open question whether we can ever hope to grasp the whole, and whether (as G. N. Clark once suggested) a deeper understanding may not be achieved by attempting to see one corner as it really was. And the third point that, I hope, emerges is the immense gain that comes from taking a wider view. I should be the last to decry the interest in local records, or belittle the work of the local record offices, which have been an outstanding feature of English history since 1945. But it is not necessarily true that here is the easiest or widest door to the past. Like Peace, History is "indivisible"; and even the English historian, interested solely in English history, will lose much of the utmost value if he ignores the great European archives. A few years ago, I tried to demonstrate how much new material had become available to historians in Germany and Austria as a result of the post-war organisation of the English county record offices. Today, I should like to suggest the importance for English history—always prone to insularity—of archives such as those I have attempted to describe. Of many archives— the Russian state archives in Moscow, for example—I know nothing; and, even where I have worked, my knowledge is limited inevitably to certain short periods. In Barcelona, for example, I have seen nothing of the many documents dealing with the Peninsular War; and it must be left to others to speak at first hand of the archives for contemporary history, or even for the days of Metternich or Bismarck. But of the importance of the great European archives there can be no doubt. They are a legacy not merely to the nations to which they belong, but to all the peoples who, in the past, have helped to build up and to carry across the seas our European heritage.

W. L. Warren

THE PEASANTS' REVOLT OF 1381[1]

In November 1380, Lords and Commons were summoned to Northampton. It was a miserable winter; heavy rains had flooded the roads, and the business of Parliament had to be put back three days to await those who had been delayed on the journey. When Members arrived, they found good lodgings too few, fuel scarce, and the place of meeting too cramped. There was no comfort, either, to be drawn from the state of the realm.

England at the close of the fourteenth century was having to make painful adjustments to political and economic changes, the very existence of which it was loath to recognise. It was hard to have to admit that the triumphs of the late King Edward III and the Black Prince over the French had been indecisive, and harder still to recognise that French recovery now made ultimate victory for the English barely possible. Commanders in the field were doing well if they avoided defeat: but a war of aggression can be sustained only by victories. Few were yet prepared to argue aloud that the country should cut its losses in

[1] [Copyright © W. L. Warren. Originally published in two parts in *History Today*, XII (1962), pp. 845-53, and XIII (1963), pp. 44-51.]

France—and those who did courted rabid unpopularity: but the taxpayer, grumbling even at the cost of triumphs, was becoming embittered at being asked to subsidise a stalemate. There might have been more readiness to call off the struggle if England itself had suffered the horrors of war: but all the bloodshed, all the destruction, had taken place on French soil. It was with the sharpest cries of indignation, and dark suspicions of betrayal, that England in the late 1370s suffered the pinpricks of raids on the south coast. Not everyone had been impoverished by the war: indeed, many had done quite well out of it; but those who reaped the greatest profits were rarely those who bore the greatest burdens, and the net result was a distortion of the traditional structure of economic power in the country.

In its most profitable phase, the war had done something to offset and disguise a serious decline in the profitability of agriculture. In the early years of the century, it had been difficult not to make substantial profits out of producing foodstuffs for the market: but prices were falling sharply by the 1330s. For a time, narrowing profit margins were offset by increasing revenue from rents—for the population was at the highest peak it was to reach in the Middle Ages and the demand for land was clamorous: but the rent boom did not survive the Black Death and the steady decline in population that the persistence of plague produced. Buyers for land could still be found who valued the prestige and local power to be derived from landholding: but marginal land was going out of cultivation, and lords often had difficulty in finding takers for vacant villein holdings—a situation unthinkable in the boom years.

Competition for increasingly scarce labour pushed up

wages. The lord who could command unpaid labour services was in an advantageous position: but no estate could be run exclusively on the customary week-work of serfs and the occasional boon-work of free tenants[2], and those (chiefly lesser lords), who were dependent on farm workers retained full time and on casual day-labourers, were faced with crisis. It was the smaller landholders— strongly represented in the Commons—who were most insistent on legislation to peg wages, such as the Statute of Labourers of 1351. But it was not always in the interests of landlords to abide by legislation that had the effect of putting all employers on the same footing when competing for labour, and despite vigorous attempts now and again and here and there to enforce the Statute, there is no doubt that it was often evaded and in the long run ineffective.

Politically, the country had been floundering for ten years—or so it seemed to Parliaments that had to listen to one excuse after another for the disappearance of taxes. King Edward III had gone into virtual retirement after 1369, and on his death in 1377 had been succeeded by his grandson, Richard II, who was then only ten years of age. It had been an unfortunate feature of the old King's declining years that his eldest son, the Black Prince, had been laid low by a recurrent sickness (he died in 1376). The prosecution of the war with France and a controlling influence in the affairs of the government at home had therefore fallen to the King's second surviving son, John of Gaunt, Duke of Lancaster. Lancaster worked loyally for the welfare of the monarchy and the realm according to

---

[2] ["Boon-works" were special services required when it was necessary to utilise every available source of labour, as at harvest.]

his lights, but he lacked his father's gift for taking the nation into his confidence, and made enemies too readily. His failure to secure a victory in France, and his inclination towards a truce, created rivals for military leadership among the nobles; his attempts to bully the clergy into releasing more of their wealth brought him diehard opponents among the upholders of clerical privilege; his moves to deprive a turbulent London of its independence provoked the bitter hostility of its citizens; and the misdeeds of Ministers for whom he shouldered responsibility earned him the deep suspicion of the Commons. People were even ready to believe that he had designs upon the throne.

In these circumstances it was unthinkable that Lancaster should act as regent for his young nephew. Instead, the Government was entrusted to a "continual council" of fluctuating membership, carefully constructed to balance rival interests. But the counsellors did not bring great credit on themselves, and the early years of Richard's reign were marked by failure abroad, scandals at home, and desperate appeals for the grant of more taxes by Parliament. By January 1380, the Commons had had enough and through their Speaker demanded an end to the continual council, the appointment of the chief officers of the Crown in Parliament, and an investigation into the operations of Government by a committee of enquiry. The Archbishop of Canterbury, Simon Sudbury, offered to take upon himself the key administrative office of Chancellor, and this was so well received by the Commons that changes in the other offices were not pressed. Sudbury had steered clear of political factions, possessed highly respected abilities, and was known as a man who could combine firmness with tact. Whether he could handle the Government's desperate situation, however, was another matter, and it soon became apparent that without fresh taxation the King's government could not be carried on at all. It was in these circumstances that Parliament was summoned in November 1380 to Northampton—not, as was becoming customary, to Westminster because of a dispute between Lancaster and the Londoners.

Only after a protracted debate did the Commons agree to a grant, and then in the generally obnoxious form of a poll tax. An earlier poll tax had been graduated according to the circumstances of the taxpayer: but this time a high flat-rate of three groats per head was fixed upon with only a vague reference to the wealthy helping the poor.

This bad business was made far worse by administrative bungling. Collecting poll taxes was a complicated and arduous business, but the desperate financial situation betrayed the Government into clumsy haste. The country was divided into convenient areas and committees appointed to each of them to assess and collect the tax, supervised and checked by small groups of "controllers". The committees were badly chosen and showed reluctance to act; many of those nominated had soon to be released because of age, infirmity, sickness, or other business; and their colleagues refused to continue work until the committees were made up to full strength again. The end of January had been fixed for paying two-thirds of the tax and Whitsuntide for the remainder: but the amounts that came in were pitifully small, and by February the Government was clamouring for the whole to be paid at once. It was still clamouring in April. Moreover, the early returns revealed that liability was being avoided on a startling scale. In a panic, the Government ordered all sheriffs and escheators to make a census of the taxable population "without waiting for or in any way communicating with the collectors and controllers", and to have the results in by Easter. But it was no use piling such an enormous task on already over-burdened officials; other persons had to be appointed to help them, but little got done. The Government wanted to blame the collectors for having "spared many persons"; but it was just not recognising the difficulty of taking particulars from an obstinate and irate population. The assessors for London pleaded that they did not dare to enquire too closely into the rank and condition of everyone, and had to be let off with putting in a rough estimate of numbers. Meanwhile, the business of collection had fallen far behind schedule. In desperation, the Government set up *ad hoc* commissions of enquiry, some in March and some at the beginning of May, for fifteen counties, and appointed a Sergeant-at-arms of the King's household to serve on each commission. The commissioners' duties, in effect, were to examine all accounts, make yet another census, and to arrest and imprison all defaulters. Some of the commissioners seem to have resorted to strong-arm methods, and their purpose was so misunderstood that people believed a completely new tax was being demanded. It is significant that the Revolt occurred in many of the counties where the commissions operated, and even more striking that no serious rising took place where they did not.

The conflicting accounts of the chroniclers do not make

it easy to establish the origins of the Revolt: but it seems
to have begun with incidents that were in themselves of
little importance, to have generated quite slowly, and then
suddenly to have burst into consuming flame. There are
signs that during May passive resistance was going over to
overt defiance. Three villages near Brentwood in Essex
got into trouble with one of the tax commissioners. The
Chief Justice of the King's Bench was sent down to hold
an enquiry and punish the offenders, but he and his small
escort were set upon and sent packing. The villagers, as if
recognising that they had now overstepped the mark,
appealed for support to their neighbours; and insurrection
rapidly engulfed the county. Across the Thames, a similar
incident involving John Legge, the King's Sergeant-at-
arms with the local commissioners, sparked off a general
rising in Kent. At Maidstone the rebels found themselves a
leader in Wat Tyler, and freed from the Archbishop's
prison a notorious rabble rouser, the vagrant priest John
Ball. Remarkably little is known of Tyler. It is possible,
though the sources of information are not above suspicion, that he was a junior member of the respectable
Culpepper family who had seen service in the French war
and had latterly taken to robbery. He certainly possessed a
gift for leadership. Contact was established with the Essex
rebels on the other side of the Thames, and on Tuesday,
11 June, the great march to London began.

The royal household hurried up from Windsor to
London at the first news of the rising, but the Government
seems to have been thoroughly disconcerted by the startling turn of events and no measures at all were taken for
coping with the situation beyond sending out messengers

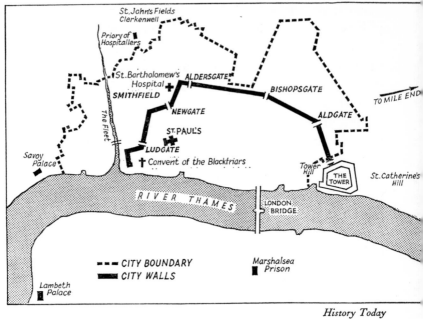

History Today

The City of London and its Surroundings at the time of
the rebels' march in June 1381.

to enquire the rebels' purpose. They replied that they wished to remove traitors to the King and the kingdom and asked for a chance to parley with him at Blackheath. On the morning of Thursday, 13 June, the young King (he was now fourteen) and his chief Ministers boarded boats at the Tower and were rowed down river to Greenwich where rebels crowded the banks. He hailed them, and they clamoured for him to land, but his advisers feared for his safety and the boats pulled away upstream again to jeers, catcalls, and threats. If the Ministers had been unnerved by the sight of thousands of militant rebels, they had even more cause for alarm when it was revealed who they meant by "traitors": a petition was brought in from the men of Kent demanding the heads of the Duke of Lancaster and fifteen other Lords and Ministers. Lancaster was safely out of the way, on a diplomatic mission to the Scottish court, but several of the others, including the Chancellor, Archbishop Sudbury, and the Treasurer, Robert Hales, who was Prior of the Knights of St John (the Hospitallers), were with the King.

Frustrated in their desire to speak with the King, the rebels surged on towards London. There was some thought in the city of closing the gates against them: but the rebels had overwhelming support among the urban proletariat and the attempt was in vain. The Kentishmen broke open the Marshalsea prison at Southwark, ransacked the Archbishop's Palace at Lambeth and then marched into the city over London Bridge to attack the property of other unpopular persons. The Londoners themselves made a special point of sacking the Duke of Lancaster's palace of the Savoy. It was done with great thoroughness and a man, it is said, who was observed making off with a piece of loot was himself thrown on to the flames.

The chroniclers have many hard words for the Government's failure to take resolute action: but by the time the rebels had been allowed to converge on London in vast numbers—and they did so with remarkable rapidity—it was a moot point whether the use of force was any longer practicable. The King's Council seems to have been divided on the issue: some were for an immediate showdown, but others argued that the only sensible policy was to wait for the inevitable break-up of the rebel hosts and to encourage it by conciliation. In the Tower on the Thursday night, as flames rose over the city, the King pressed his Council for clear advice, but none was forthcoming, and it was on his own initiative, so it is said, that proclamation was made throughout the city that everyone should go on the morrow to Mile End, where he would speak with them.

Mile End was chosen as the meeting place, partly in the hope that it would draw the rebels away from the Tower and enable the wanted men to escape. But the rebels were not so easily duped and stationed a strong detachment opposite the Tower on St Catherine's Hill. (Archbishop Sudbury did make the attempt to get away by boat but was spotted by a "wicked woman" and had to retreat hastily.) The meeting at Mile End went off peaceably: the rebels were courteous and the King placatory. They could have their way with any traitors, he said, if their treachery had been proved by legal process, and he would grant all they desired in the way of freedom from the burdens of serfdom. Clerks were set to work immediately drawing up charters. During the King's absence, however, a party of rebels, under the leadership it seems of Tyler himself, had broken into the Tower (how they did so remains one of the mysteries of the Revolt). They did little damage; all they wanted were the "traitors". Sudbury, Hales, John Legge, and a friar whose only guilt was that he was physician to the Duke of Lancaster, were dragged out and clumsily beheaded.

With the supposed treachery avenged, and with charters of freedom in their hands, many of the rebels began to disperse to their homes—but not all of them. That Friday night, the city and suburbs were again given over to wild disorder. It is not certain who of the rebels remained. Some historians hold that the Mile End meeting was attended only by the men of Essex, others that it met the grievances only of the upper and middle ranks of the peasantry, and yet others that it did not satisfy the radical aims of a more militant section of the rebels. Evidence can be adduced in support of each of these views: but whatever the reason, a further meeting was held at Smithfield on the Saturday.

The Smithfield meeting is probably the best known episode of the Revolt, even though the conflicting accounts of the chroniclers make it difficult to ascertain precisely what happened. Richard, it seems, was determined to pursue the policy that had paid dividends already and concede any demands that might be made, but Tyler was reluctant to accept the King's promises. His truculence turned to insolence, Mayor Walworth became angry, tempers flared, and Tyler was struck to the ground. It was a desperate moment, for the whole royal party could have been butchered, and it says much for the courage of the young King that he spurred his horse towards the rebels crying, "Sirs, will you shoot your King? I will be your captain; follow me." They followed him: but whether Richard would survive was still an open question as he led them away to St John's Fields at Clerkenwell. Some of the royal party, it is said, fled the scene "for fear that they had of an affray". Mayor Walworth rode back hurriedly into the city to call upon the aldermen to turn out the loyal citizens of their wards and the garrison of the Tower. But the turning point had been reached: by the time the troops and armed citizens came up to the King at Clerkenwell, the rebels wanted nothing but to be allowed to return to their homes.

Much less well-known, and for the most part much less well chronicled, is the course of the Revolt outside London. It spread partly by contagion from the original centres of insurrection, and partly by the efforts of enthusiastic emissaries who travelled considerable distances to bring stirring tales of what was happening in London. It was only in the home counties and eastern England, however, that rebellion spread generally. Middlesex and north Surrey were drawn into the events of the city: but elsewhere the Revolt took on a marked local character—a fact that handicaps attempts at generalisation.

Some of the sharpest conflicts took place in towns—usually quite independently of risings of the peasantry. Indeed, some town riots occurred in areas where the peasantry remained quiescent—York, Scarborough, Beverley, and Winchester are cases in point. Reports of a breakdown of law and order were sufficient to induce

them, it may be suspected, not the circulation of re-
volutionary ideas. For the most part they were revolts
against the privileges of a ruling clique; but in each case
the character of the strife was determined by the town's
distinctive history. In some cases, at Beverley and Winchester, for example, artisans and small tradesmen rose
against oligarchies of rich merchants; in others, notably at
St Albans, Peterborough, Dunstable, and, more con-
fusedly, at Bury St Edmunds, the townsmen were more
or less united in opposition to the seigneurial authority
exercised over the town by a great abbey. At York, however, the trouble seems to have been a struggle between
factions undifferentiated by class divisions; and, at Cambridge, the disturbances inevitably took the form of town
versus gown. For some of the towns the riot of June 1381
was but an incident in a long history of violent disturbances: at St Albans, for example, there had been
serious trouble in 1274, 1314, and 1326.

The character of the local peasant revolts was determined by the kind of leadership they received, if any. In
west Norfolk, no leader of note emerged, and the story is
one of sporadic disturbances on a village scale. In west
Suffolk, a certain John Wrawe achieved great fame for
himself as "King of the Commons" and organised daring
raids in the countryside around Bury St Edmunds: but he
seems to have been little more than a rogue exploiting
genuine grievances for his own aggrandisement and
profit. A curious feature of the Revolt, in several other
parts of the eastern counties, is the participation of members of the gentry. It may be supposed that they were
moved by private grievances to take advantage of the

situation—for the recovery of property lost at law, or the settlement of old scores, it may be: but in the absence of positive evidence, speculation is idle.

In east Norfolk, the peasants had the active co-operation of two knights, Sir Roger Bacon and Sir Thomas Cornerd, and the enforced adherence (so they claimed) of several more: but the insurrection there is remarkable on other counts. It found a leader of ability in Geoffrey Litster, a dyer of Felmingham. The rebels were assembled at the ancient meeting place of the shire on Mousehold Heath, and marched on Norwich where the burgesses were overawed into opening the gates. Litster was installed in state at the castle, and sent out detachments charged with the task of destroying manorial records and arresting "traitors". Litster sometimes himself went down to supervise the work and sat in judgment on cases of disputed property. Indiscriminate pillage, it seems, was checked. Sir Roger Bacon led a force to Yarmouth, whose privileges were much resented by the neighbouring countryside, tore up the town's charter and set up new customs officers to receive the charges that were formerly paid to the town. It is possible that Litster intended only the satisfaction of long-standing grievances: but it seems more likely that he had in mind a grand plan for provincial self-government, based on the support of the "true commons" (as the rebels liked to call themselves), but quite ready to respect and enlist the help of sympathetic landlords. One of his first moves had been to try to recruit the co-operation of the Earl of Suffolk, who was then staying at one of his manors in the county; but the Earl, hearing that a party of rebels was looking for him, rose from his dinner and fled across

country. But Litster's efforts were only beginning as the
rebellion in the south-east was drawing to its close, and by
20 June he seems to have decided that little could be hoped
for beyond a general pardon for his followers and a charter
for the county similar to the ones granted at Mile End. He
despatched envoys to seek out the King, but they got no
further than Newmarket before being intercepted and
arrested. Rebellion was giving way to repression.

The general failure of those whose interests were
threatened to oppose the Revolt locally is explicable only
in terms of panic. That resistance was possible is shown by
the exceptional instances. At Huntingdon, a junior clerk
of the royal Chancery rallied some neighbours and beat
off a party of rebels who were returning from London,
then gathered forces from the local gentry and dispersed
the rebels who were terrorising the Abbot of Ramsey.
Henry Despenser, the aristocratic Bishop of Norwich, took
action on his own initiative on a bigger scale. He was
returning to his diocese from Rutland with only a few
armed retainers when he heard of the rising against the
abbey of Peterborough. Calling to him some of the local
gentry, he fell upon the town and sent the rebels scurrying.
Then, gathering strength as he went, he moved swiftly
from one centre of revolt to another, hanging some
leaders on the spot and arresting others, as far south as
Cambridge. It was into his hands that Litster's envoys fell,
and learning of what was happening in his diocese, he set
out for Norwich at the head of what was by now a considerable force. At his coming Litster fell back, hurriedly
gathering his scattered followers. At North Walsham, he
decided to make a stand and fortified a position with a

ditch and palisade, protecting his rear by chaining his wagons wheel to wheel[2]. But the Bishop, without hesitation, carried the defences in a frontal assault, himself in the lead. Litster was captured and promptly hanged.

Meanwhile, the Government had gone over to the offensive in the south-east. A series of proclamations called upon local officials to establish order, roundly denied rumours that the King was a party to or sympathised with the activities of the rebels, and enjoined all loyal men to arrest any rebels found under arms. The Essex men had dispersed from Mile End confident in the promises they had received, but now they became alarmed. Some who sought confirmation of their charters from the King were abused, and told that no value could be put on pledges extorted by force. Open insurrection flared up again, but this time the Government was ready for it, and a rebel army was cut down by a royal force at Billericay. From Chelmsford on 2 July the King announced that by the advice of his Council he had annulled the charters "lately granted in haste". Rumblings of discontent and local defiance continued for a long time, but never again on a scale to threaten the preservation of order.

Some historians have been inclined to minimise the political aspects of the Revolt, but only against the grain of the evidence. Contemporaries were well aware of its political implications, and critics of the Government for some years afterwards called attention to them. In the Parliament that met in November 1381, a Suffolk knight

[3] [In the second and third decades of the fifteenth century the Hussite armies in Bohemia used the same technique with success, and employed it offensively. They also were a largely proletarian force.]

attributed the rising to the extravagance of the court, the lack of firm direction in the administration, the burden of taxation, and the poor state of the country's defences. In the Parliament of 1383, Michael de la Pole, speaking as the newly appointed Chancellor, held that hostility towards the lesser officials of the Crown such as sheriffs, escheators, and tax collectors was "the source and principal cause of the traitorous insurrection". No doubt, it was comforting to have the blame laid elsewhere than on the landholding classes: but such comments gained substance from what had happened during the Revolt. The people who suffered physical violence at the hands of the rebels had been officials of the Crown (at all levels), members of the gentry who were implicated in the operations of government (as local justices, for instance), and lawyers. In striking contrast, landlords who had no part in such unpopular activities were left, for the most part, unmolested.

The pursuit of "traitors"—those held responsible for the long tale of governmental failure—was relentless. As the Kentishmen marched on London, they had replied to the King's messengers that they had risen to save him and the kingdom from traitors. The handing over of traitors was the first of the demands laid before the King at Mile End. In Kent, Essex, and London a special object was the destruction of property belonging to the Duke of Lancaster, Archbishop Sudbury, Prior Hales, and other Ministers. One of Lancaster's servants was badly beaten up in Kent "because of the hatred they had for the Duke". Political consciousness was probably at its greatest in London and contiguous counties, but more distant areas can show examples of the same kind of thing. The first sign of trouble in Cambridgeshire was an attack on the property of the Hospitallers. Leaders of risings in the county, both north and south, claimed to hold commissions from the King to destroy traitors. The only sign of trouble in Leicestershire was the burning of the Hospitallers' tithe barns. Rumour was rife in Leicester itself that rebels were coming to destroy property belonging to the Duke of Lancaster. During the strife between town and gown in Cambridge, Corpus Christi College was sacked because it was "of the patronage of the King's uncle, the Duke of Lancaster". In north-west Norfolk, a royal justice and a steward of the Duke took to a small open boat to avoid the fury of the rebels, were hotly pursued out to sea and only made good their escape under cover of darkness. At Lynn there was a demonstration against "traitors" and several persons were cast into prison. Such instances could be readily multiplied.

It is possible that the peasantry was conscious of political isolation. During the century, the gentry had been increasingly drawn into the orbit of the old governing classes and the mechanism of central government, as members both of Parliament and of the local commissions that administered legislation and kept the peace. At the same time, those institutions of the community that were known and understood, the manor, the vill, and the shire, counted for much less than of old. Some feeling that they had been deserted by the gentry, and that the Commons in Parliament spoke for only sectional interests, may lie behind the rebels' frequent insistence that they were the "true commons" on whose loyalty the King could depend. It is possible, too, that some at least of the lesser gentry

who joined the rebels did so for reasons of political dis-
satisfaction, seeing the Revolt—and perhaps not altogether mistakenly—as a political demonstration rather
than an episode in a class war.

Political grievances, though, remain the most obscure
aspect of the Revolt for they never achieved articulate
expression. The rebels' political aspirations were indeed
very unsophisticated—the hounding of "traitors" is the
crudest form of political activity: but it can hardly be
denied that politics was the unifying factor for diverse
groups of rebels, and the driving force for the remarkable
march on London. It may well be that the explosion would
not have occurred had it not been for the long tale of
governmental failure, the oppressive burden of taxation
that it involved, and the clumsiness of an incompetent
administration so clearly revealed in the attempts to
collect the poll tax. But politics, of course, were not the
whole of the story.

It is easy to assume that the peasants who rose in revolt
were men exasperated by the misery of their condition,
reduced to penury by punitive taxation, and crushed by the
attempts of lords to exact the full rigour of manorial
servitude. But if this were so it would be a matter for sur-
prise that the Revolt was confined to areas that were
among the most prosperous in the country. In fact, a
prominent part seems to have been taken in the risings by
men who were comparatively well to do. Take, for
instance, Thomas Sampson, who held land in Kersey and
Harkstead and led the rising in south-east Suffolk. A man
of apparently humble origins, he had acquired some half-
dozen peasant holdings, run as separate units, but totalling

some one hundred and eighty acres. He had enterprisingly gone in for grazing and kept fifteen cows with a bull, a hundred hogs, and a flock of three hundred sheep producing fine wool for the clothiers. He had invested his surplus profit in an eighth share of a vessel berthed at Harwich. He dined off pewter, had several pieces of silver, and some fine earthenware and linen.

In the years after the Black Death it was perfectly possible for peasants with enterprise and a fair measure of luck to prosper, for the plague, though it caused many thousands of personal tragedies, opened up possibilities of a new life for the survivors. It removed at a stroke one of the principal causes of rural poverty: an expanding population struggling to subsist on too little cultivable land. Much peasant prosperity of later days must have owed its origin to a profitable marriage with a widow and an undertaking to work the vacant holdings of deceased neighbours in the 1350s. But as soon as possibilities opened to the peasant, his social superiors conspired, or so it must have seemed, to hold him down. As he strove to become a commodity producer for the market, his lord, himself facing adverse conditions, stepped up rents. As the serf aspired to buy himself out of servitude, he found the bonds of the manor tightening around him, for the lord could no longer afford to let slip any of the profitable jurisdiction of the manorial court. (On the manor of Hulton in Essex, fines in the manorial court trebled in the '60s[4].) Taxes of unheard of frequency crippled his enterprise. Perhaps such taxes were at least endurable when everyone, rich and poor,

---

[4] [Fines included a down-payment to a lord on succession to a tenement or when one was alienated or surrendered.]

free and unfree, paid in proportion to his means, but in November 1380 the Commons had stooped to the iniquitous device of a flat-rate tax per head of the population. (One of the earliest cries to which the rebels gave voice was for no more taxes "except the fifteenths which their fathers and forebears knew and accepted".)

Quite apart from this aspect of the situation, however, the villein who by hard work had achieved a new standard of living was just the one who would feel most bitter about the law's insistence on his servile origins. Even if his standard of living could bear comparison with that of local free peasants and the lesser gentry; even if he could afford to hire substitutes to perform the menial tasks that manorial custom required of him; even if his lord were a decent enough man who had helped the family, as he should, in bad times, who was glad to see a tenant prosper and exacted no more from his prosperity than reasonable custom allowed—even so, such a peasant would daily be conscious of disabilities that stemmed from nothing but his legal status. As a serf, he was debarred from ever being able to defend his interests at the regular meetings of the shire; he could have no say in the election of men who would agree to taxes in Parliament; he could never aspire to the ranks of the local magistracy which virtually ran the country in the name of the Government. If he ran into legal difficulties over his land holdings (as was very likely), he could not resort to the quick remedies that kings had provided, for the royal courts were open only to freemen. He could never become a burgess of the town where he marketed his produce, share the privileges of its corporation, or help fix the regulations that controlled its markets and tolls. He could not marry his children to their best advantage (and his).

There was no point in telling such a man that this is how the world was and always would be, and that he should bear his unfortunate lot with at least as much patience as his father had done; for he could see around him the clearest signs that the kind of society he had been born into was not inevitable or immutable. Lords had reacted to the economic conditions in different ways. While some tightened up their exactions of villein services, others preferred to become *rentiers*, leasing their demesne lands, commuting labour services to money rents, and selling villeins their freedom. Hence, on neighbouring manors, the condition of the peasantry might be radically different. And even under the same lord, there might be no uniformity of practice, for prudent lords would rationalise the administration of their estates, retaining the old methods where they could be worked conveniently and economically, but commuting villein services and leasing demesne on scattered, distant, or less profitable manors. Besides feeling the exasperation of such anomalies, the villein had to witness the sudden rise to good fortune of the class below him—the landless labourers (previously the most lowly element of the rural population), who could now contract for service with the highest bidder and bargain for the abolition of anything that still marked them out as bondsmen. Inevitably, the consequence of such developments was an upheaval in the social structure of the village community; and it would not be surprising if the Revolt embraced something of a Poujadist element. Those who rebelled had noticeably little to say about the

Statute of Labourers. But, before the Revolt broke out,
villeins had been responding to the situation in the only
way open to them: deserting their holdings and fleeing to
distant parts where they could take work as wage
labourers with no questions asked. There is something
very wrong when a peasant will abandon his land.

For the class immediately above the villein, that of the
ordinary freeman, the opportunities in the late fourteenth
century were such that the bond-man might see nothing
standing between himself and his highest ambitions but his
servitude. In the heart of the rebellious area, at Sudbury
in Suffolk, a stained glass window had recently been
erected to the memory of Nigel Thebaud and his wife.
The Thebauds were an old but hardly exalted Sudbury
family—indeed, their only claim to distinction was a possible distant kinship to a knight. But Nigel Thebaud was
enterprising and flourished as a trader to Sudbury and
district, supplying the local nobility and gentry with luxury
goods, and acting as a middleman for the developing cloth
trade. He was able to set up his oldest son, John, with a
little land over the Essex border near to Sudbury. John
increased his capital by acting as a small-time financier,
bought more land, married quite well, enlarged his house,
and could number himself among the lesser gentry.
Indeed, he was asked to serve on numerous judicial commissions, and twice represented his county in Parliament.
Nigel married his third son, while he was still very young,
into a family of Ipswich burgesses and set him up there as a
merchant. Robert made his mark as a shipper: in the 1350s
he was hiring vessels to take corn to Holland and Zeeland,
and by the '60s he was sending a ship of his own down to

Britanny for salt, and dealing in goods from Gascony and
Spain. He, too, attended Parliament as one of the Members returned by the borough of Ipswich in 1366. Nigel
Thebaud's second son, Simon, was destined for the Church.
As a boy of ability, he was brought to the notice of local
patrons and sent to the Schools. There his ability proved
exceptional, and he embarked on a career as an ecclesiastical
lawyer, which took him from the service of the Bishop of
Norwich to the exalted office of a judge in the papal court
at Avignon. In 1362 he came back to England to be Bishop
of London at the Pope's nomination. In 1375 he became
Archbishop of Canterbury, and in 1380 Chancellor of
England, for he was that same Simon "of Sudbury" whose
head was hacked off on Tower Hill on 14 June 1381.

Apart from the exceptional case of Simon, the prosper-
ing of Nigel Thebaud and his sons could be emulated by
the humblest man, provided he had energy and enterprise
—and provided, of course, he were not shackled to
manorial servitude. What the manorial villein lacked, and
what in the later fourteenth century he was conscious as
never before of lacking, was equality of opportunity.
Equality of opportunity was not, of course, the only cry
in 1381, but it was a prominent one that determined much
of the character of the Revolt. It comes out clearly in the
specific demands at Mile End: the abolition of serfdom,
labour services only on a basis of free contract, and the
renting of land at fourpence an acre. This was not a pro-
gramme of radical revolution: there was no demand here
for the confiscation of land or for peasant proprietorship,
or indeed, an attack upon the principle of lordship—all the
peasants were asking for, in effect, was for a chance to

A country woman, spindle under her arm, feeds the chickens.
Miniature from Luttrell Psalter, *c.* 1340.

PLATE OVERLEAF

(*Left*) Wat Tyler is slain as he threatens the King at
Smithfield. (*Right*) Richard II presents himself to the
rebels as their leader. Miniature from a contemporary
manuscript of Froissart's *Chronicle*.

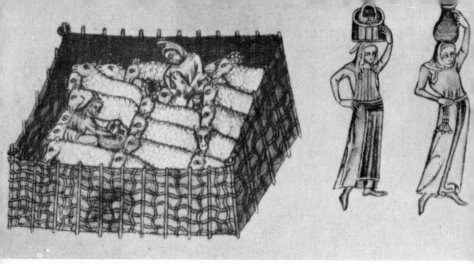

Peasant tending sheep.   Miniature from Luttrell Psalter, *c.* 1340.

make their own way in the world. The villein of 1381 found himself trapped inside the shell of an obsolescent society from which nearly everyone except himself seemed to be escaping. He did not attack his landlord personally, he attacked the shell: from every corner of the area in revolt come stories of the burning of manorial records, and attacks upon members of the legal profession because they groped in the past for evidence of old customs and obligations instead of opening doors into the future.

Others who felt themselves trapped were the inhabitants of towns under seigneurial lordship. Of the rising at St Albans against its lord, the Abbot of the great Benedictine monastery, we are particularly well informed, for the chronicler Thomas Walsingham was a monk there and wrote with first-hand knowledge of the events he described. Walsingham not unnaturally vilifies the rebels, but it is possible, even so, to see that they were moved by a spirit similar to that of the rebels at Mile End, though of course the specific demands of the townsfolk were different from those of the peasantry. St Albans was a thriving market town which would long since have achieved municipal autonomy if it had had any other lord but autocratic Abbots, who believed it their duty to keep the town in a state of manorial dependence, and appropriated all profitable right to the monastery. There was a long history of strife against the Abbot's authority; but the forces of law and order had always intervened on the side of the lord, though the townsmen stoutly maintained that King Offa had granted a charter to their ancestors which the monks had stolen. It would not have been surprising if they had seized the opportunity of the anarchy of the June days of 1381 to vent their pent-up emotions in doing violence to the monks and sacking the abbey: but they kept any tendencies towards indiscriminate violence in check, like the peasants who distinguished between the person of their lord and his manorial records. The townsmen were prepared to use force, but only to the extent necessary to secure concessions that were in themselves moderate. The Abbot was notoriously hard-bitten and not easily intimidated: but the townsmen, under the leadership of William Grindcob, brought pressure to bear on him by destroying one by one and step by step the symbols of his seigneurial privileges. First they broke down the gates of the abbey's home farm, then they uprooted the hedges that protected its coverts, drained its fish-ponds, broke open its prison and sat in judgement on the inmates (sentencing a notorious malefactor to be hanged and setting the rest free). Next they destroyed the charters that defined the abbey's privileges and its manorial records. Then they took up the millstones which an earlier Abbot had seized from the townsmen (to prevent them grinding their own corn free of the abbey's tolls) and had used as floor paving for his parlour. Meanwhile, a deputation of townsmen had gone down to London and had prudently conferred with both the King and Wat Tyler. From the one they brought back a letter to the Abbot and from the other a promise of support. At last the Abbot gave way. Since he could not produce the charter supposedly granted by King Offa, the townsmen framed another for him to seal. What they demanded were rights of pasturage, freedom to take game, the abolition of the seigneurial mill, and the concession of freedom to the town to govern itself by elected officers. No violence had been done to the monks and no serious damage to the fabric of the abbey itself. What the townsmen were seeking, in short, was equality of opportunity with towns of comparable size, and what they attacked were simply artificial limitations on their freedom of enterprise.

The men of St Albans were very reluctant to abandon their gains, and continued their defiance even when the Revolt was in full retreat elsewhere. Grindcob had been arrested in the first flush of reaction, but was later released on bail to see if he could redeem himself by calling his friends to order. Instead, he chose to put fresh heart into them with a speech that reads well even from the bitterly hostile pen of Walsingham: "Friends", he said, "whom a little liberty has refreshed after so long an oppression, stand fast while you can, and take no thought for what I may suffer; for if in the cause of liberty I must die, I shall think myself happy to end my days as a martyr". He was hanged.

Of course, this was not the only spirit abroad in the Revolt. Inarticulate peasants, who could not formulate their grievances and had no leader who could do it for them, were doubtless often brought to venting their bitterness in senseless violence. The surprising thing is that this was not the common case. Then again, there were wilder men who pushed themselves to the fore and sought to take command of the rebels for their own darker purposes. Such men might be mere desperadoes like John Wrawe in west Suffolk, or somewhat demented like John Ball, who seems to have cherished wild schemes for the replacement of the whole ecclesiastical hierarchy by himself. Too much should not be made of the "socialism" of the famous sermon which he is said to have preached to the Kentish men on the theme

> When Adam dalf and Eve span
> Who was then a gentleman?

Such sentiments were the stock in trade of medieval itinerant preachers. It was for slander that Ball had been imprisoned, not sedition.

Wat Tyler has obtained a secure niche for himself in the folk-lore of English history, but what little we know of him does not suggest that he deserves it as much as Grindcob of St Albans or Litster of Norfolk. It is doubtful, for one thing, if he represented the true interests of the men he led. One of his henchmen, Jack Straw, is alleged to have made a confession before his execution, in which he said that Tyler's plan was to seize the King, and hold him as hostage while they executed the leading magnates and confiscated Church property. "And when no one survived who was greater or stronger or more learned than ourselves we would have made whatever laws we liked." Ultimately, the King would have been killed and the realm divided up among the rebel chieftains. It is difficult to say how much credence can be put in this story; but, if it were true, it would help to explain Tyler's behaviour at the Smithfield meeting. If he were more interested in perpetuating his own power than in securing fair treatment for the men he led, then the King's conciliatory attitude at the Mile End meeting would have been very disturbing to him. To counteract the rebels' instinctive loyalty to the King and their readiness to be content with grants of charters (now that the "traitors" had been hounded to death), he would have to provoke the Government into revealing its true hostility to the rising. Hence, it may be, the extravagance of many of his demands at Smithfield, including the end of all lordship, the equalising of all men save the King, the distribution of Church property among the laity, "and that there should be only one bishop in England and only one prelate". The mild reaction of the King even to these impossible demands must have been very disconcerting; all that he could fall back on was studied insolence, and in the ensuing fracas he was mortally wounded. It may be an indication that the rebels were growing apprehensive about Tyler's leadership that they so readily left his wounded body on the ground (it was carried by his friends into St Bartholomew's Hospital) and followed Richard to Clerkenwell fields. After the King had been conversing with them for the best part of an hour, they were surrounded by armed citizens from London and Sir Robert Knolle's mercenary troops, and it was whispered to him that he might now take his vengeance; but he replied, "Three-quarters of them have been brought here by fear and intimidation; I will not have the innocent suffer with the guilty", and ordered instead that they be escorted home. Such, at any rate, is Froissart's story.

The collapse of the Revolt was followed, inevitably, by the punishment of the rebels. For a month the royal court toured Essex and Hertfordshire while the Chief Justice of the King's Bench tried offenders. Elsewhere, the Chief Justice of the Common Pleas and judicial commissions were at work. At first it seemed as if there would be a reign of terror; but by the time that the pacification of the disaffected areas had been completed by local officials, judicial savagery had given place to a proper respect for the due processes of law. Torture was not allowed; there were very few cases of conviction without the verdict of a jury, and there were quite a few acquittals of persons whose guilt seems beyond doubt; in some cases sentences were mitigated and in others pardons were granted. Parliament, meeting in November 1381, asked for a general amnesty for all except two hundred and eighty-seven serious offenders. By the time capital sentences came to an end something over a hundred had been done to death. Taken as a whole, the repression was mild in comparison with the brutal treatment the French peasants had suffered after their rising in 1358: but then, the English rising had been no *Jacquerie*.

The results of the Revolt were negligible. While some lords were prompted by it to divest themselves of manorial responsibilities, and to allow their villeins the greater opportunities of leasehold tenure, other lords clamped down with even greater severity. By and large, life in the English countryside after the Revolt went on pretty much as if it had never happened. The one positive achievement the rebels gained was to dissuade Parliament from ever again venturing a poll tax. The liberties that the rebels had sought were to come eventually, not as the result of revolution, but from the working out of economic forces that had already begun their relentless pressure before the remarkable eruption of June 1381.

J. L. Kirby

THE COUNCIL OF 1407 AND
THE PROBLEM OF CALAIS[1]

Council at London. At that time the king held a great
council at London which lasted from Easter for almost
nine weeks. About its business we were not allowed to
learn, except that the king raised money in loans from the
clergy and the laity. To what end the Lord knows.

In these words Thomas Walsingham, the last of the great
monk chroniclers of St Albans Abbey, recorded a meeting
of King Henry IV's council in the year 1407. "This
council", says the editor of the Chronicle, Professor Galbraith, "is not mentioned by Stubbs, and there seems to
be no other evidence for it." Certainly no records of its
proceedings are now known to survive, but this is not
unusual, for the council proceedings which have survived
from this period cover but a fraction of the meetings that
must have been held. Nevertheless, a great deal may be
learned about this and other meetings from casual references in the records of other bodies as well as from the
chroniclers. Indeed the problem which this particular

[1] [Copyright © J. L. Kirby. Originally published in *History Today*, v
(1955), pp. 44-52.]

session was called upon to solve, and the means by which it did so, were graphically summed up by another chronicler in the following words:

> At that time [he wrote] the king had long failed to pay the wages of the soldiers guarding Calais, wherefore they arrested the wools of the merchants which were at Calais. The merchants complained to the king, and he asked them to lend him the money. But the merchants excused themselves. 'You have the gold,' said the king, 'and I want the gold, where is it?' Finally, after much delay the merchants lent him the gold, on condition that the Chancellor, the Archbishop of Canterbury and the Duke of York guaranteed its repayment. This they did.

That then was the problem. The soldiers of the garrison at Calais were in a state bordering on mutiny, because their pay was grossly in arrears, and money had to be found to pay them. Clearly the King's credit was bad, for the merchants were only induced to lend on receiving a guarantee from the Archbishop and the Duke. In fact, although the chronicler put the words into the King's own mouth, it was the council which negotiated the loans. But this was still only a fragment of the story.

The Parliament which met at Westminster on 1 March 1406, was probably the most important and certainly the longest one of the reign if not of the whole of the Middle Ages. It sat, with long breaks at Easter and in the summer, until 22 December. The Speaker was Sir John Tiptoft, and through his mouth the Commons showed much more anxiety to criticise the King and his court than to grant supplies. Three times during the session the names of the King's Councillors were announced, on 22 May, 27

November, and 22 December, but this does not seem to have increased the confidence of the Commons in the administration. On the last occasion the Councillors were made to take a solemn oath in Parliament to observe thirty-one articles governing the conduct of their official duties; and it was only then, when most of the members must have lost all hope of getting home for Christmas, that the usual grant of a subsidy of one-fifteenth was made. This grant was payable in the middle of the following February.

Historians have remarked on the differences between the three lists of Councillors, but most of the differences were in fact due to normal promotions and changes amongst the office-holders, and the lists are really remarkably consistent. At the head of each was the Archbishop of Canterbury, Thomas Arundel. Fourteen years older than King Henry IV, Arundel at fifty-four already possessed a veteran's experience of the politics of both Church and State. A younger son and brother of the Earls of Arundel, he had been promoted Bishop of Ely at twenty-one, and had taken a leading part with the Earl, his brother, in the politics of Richard II's court. He was raised to the archbishopric of York in 1388 and translated to Canterbury in 1396, only to be deprived and exiled by Richard in the following year. Abroad, he had joined Henry of Lancaster, and returning as his leading adviser placed the royal Crown on his head in 1399.

Besides Arundel, the lists comprised two or three other bishops, including Henry Beaufort of Winchester, the King's half-brother, the Duke of York, the Earl of Somerset, another of the Beaufort brothers, two or three

F—E.S.G.

barons, the great officers of state, and (in the first list only) three knights, two of whom had served as Speakers of the Commons. The officers were the Chancellor, Thomas Langley, Bishop of Durham, the Treasurer, Lord Furnival, the Keeper of the Privy Seal, and the Steward, Chamberlain and (in the last list only) the Treasurer, of the royal household. The Steward was Sir John Stanley, and not, as has usually been assumed, Prince Thomas, the King's second son, who bore the honorary dignity of Steward of England. To this group of about fifteen magnates the day to day supervision of the business of the kingdom was entrusted.

The first happening of importance in 1407 took place at Westminster on 30 January. In the presence of the King, Thomas Langley gave up the great seal, and Archbishop Arundel was made Chancellor in his place. Perhaps Langley, who had been appointed Bishop of Durham less than six months before, wished to devote some time to the affairs of his see, but whatever the reason the change clearly placed Arundel in a very strong position. Already the senior member of the Council, he now became the King's first minister also, a combination of duties which can only be compared with those of a modern prime minister. A fortnight later the Archbishop was at his palace at Lambeth, and on 19 February, the Council met at Westminster to discuss a petition from the City of London. This was the only meeting of the Council held in 1407 for which any record of the proceedings has survived. The subsidy granted in Parliament in December was now due and by the beginning of March £25,000 was paid into the Exchequer in cash, but even so the Exchequer found it necessary to borrow £900 from the Earl of Westmorland, and £200 from Thomas Knolles, a London merchant. The financial situation was already critical. The revenue, including the sums arising from the last Parliamentary grant, barely sufficed to meet current needs and, at the same time, the experience of the previous year did not suggest that it would be much use to summon another Parliament and ask for more money. The alternative was to borrow on a large scale, but the possible lenders must have been quite well aware of the Exchequer's difficulties, which made early repayment unlikely.

It was probably at this moment that the Archbishop and the Council learnt of the events at Calais. The wages of the garrison had been grossly in arrears for several years, and now the soldiers seized the wool which was waiting in the merchants' warehouses to be sold to the Flemings. It was the only form of wealth on which they could lay their hands. On 9 March, Robert Thorley, the Treasurer of Calais, that is the paymaster of the forces there, was replaced by Richard Merlawe, a London merchant. This was apparently the first action taken by the Council, and was probably directed to appeasing both the soldiers, by making the Treasurer a scapegoat, and the merchants, by making one of their number responsible for the finances of Calais.

It is said that the Emperor Sigismund, visiting Henry V a few years after these events, stressed the importance of Calais to the English Crown, and

> "a jewel most of alle
> in Latyn did it calle".

Since Sigismund was a very distinguished guest, the English King and his Council no doubt listened politely, but it was not news to them, for Calais occupied a key position in the finances and the defences of England at that time, with the result, that the defence of Calais and its cost were constantly recurring items on the agenda of the Council.

When in 1347 Edward III had captured Calais, and entered it with solemn pageantry, he was determined to convert it into an English town, a little bit of England beyond the sea. He expelled a large part of the French population, and issued proclamations in England offering the vacant houses to English people willing to settle in the town. If this policy of anglicisation was only partially successful at least Calais was kept. From Calais, King Edward marched his conquering armies across France: but when he died thirty years later, unrespected and un-regretted, Crecy and Poitiers were but memories. His famous son, Edward the Black Prince, was already dead; and of all their conquests in France, Calais, with its march now shrunken to two small lordships, alone remained to be handed down to the Councillors of that unfortunate boy, Richard II. Thus, perhaps Calais became a symbol, a memorial of all that was won and lost, and a reminder that Edward III's claim to the throne of France was not abandoned. For another hundred years the idea of con-quering France was not allowed to die, and Calais was carefully guarded not only as a pledge to the memory of Edward III, but also, more practically, as a convenient gateway to France, as a foothold from which a new conquest might begin.

In addition to this use as a possible military base, the town had been given another function. After several experiments in regulating the wool-trade, Edward III fixed the staple at Calais in 1363. The export of wool was then England's largest trade, and the money which it brought in was the only readily accessible form of wealth both for taxation and for borrowing. Edward gave a monopoly of the trade to a company of the larger merchants engaged in it, on condition that all their wool was taken to Calais and sold there. This regulation, by confining the trade to a single channel, facilitated the collection of a large subsidy or export duty at the English ports; and also concentrated the cash received for the sale of wool into the hands of a group of merchants, who could be called upon to lend it to the King when the occasion arose. Since the wool subsidy provided a large part of the revenues of the Kings of England, and the garrison of Calais absorbed an almost equally large part of their expenditure, it was a natural step to link the two together. Hence a part of the subsidy on wool came to be regularly earmarked for the garrison of Calais. The fact that this garrison was effectively guarding the market where the wool was sold brought the two still closer; and, by the employment of a simple system of credit, it was possible to pay the troops with the actual cash received by the merchants, and to avoid the transport of bullion to and from England. Unfortunately, the system could only be worked if the Exchequer had ample credit and cash for the King's current expenses in England, and this was but rarely the case in the fifteenth century.

In order to defend Calais, it was necessary to maintain

a strong permanent garrison there. The establishment was fixed at about 800 men in time of peace and 1,000 in war. Of the peace establishment, 460 were stationed in the town under the direct command of the Captain of Calais. The Treasurer of Calais had a personal escort of twenty more, and two other parties of the same strength were stationed in the Castle of Calais and in a tower by the port. The rest were divided between four or five other castles in the march, which formed a defensive ring round the town. The largest, Guines, had a garrison of 100, and the others had about twenty or thirty men in each. Every castle had its own captain, but all were under the ultimate command of the Captain of Calais. About half of the soldiers were men-at-arms and the other half were archers. A proportion of both classes was mounted, and in time of war the proportion of horsemen was substantially increased so that the forces were more mobile.

To modern eyes this force of 1,000 men or less seems absurdly small, but in the Europe of that day it was quite unheard of to maintain a large force permanently under arms. Armies were raised for single campaigns, and then dispersed, while castles were guarded only by the household of king or lord. In practice the number of troops at Calais never reached the full establishment, but a large number were there all the time, and they had to be paid. Moreover, they had to be paid more than the normal medieval soldier, to whom booty was more important than pay. These men, who were merely occupied in guard duties, could hardly be encouraged to live off the land or to plunder. Instead, they were given a special quarterly bonus beyond their pay. Besides the troops, it was also necessary to maintain a small band of masons and labourers constantly at work in repairing and strengthening the fortifications both of Calais and of the outlying castles. Finally, most of the food and stores had to be brought from England, and for many items the cost of transport was higher than the cost of the stores themselves.

Altogether, the average cost of this garrison to the English Exchequer was at least £17,000 a year. Once again the figure does not seem large to modern eyes, but at this time the money received by the Exchequer in a single year rarely amounted to £100,000, and was usually very much less, so that the cost of Calais might be as much as one-quarter of the King's revenues. It is not difficult, therefore, to understand why the English Council was constantly made aware of the cost of the garrison at Calais.

It was at Easter, according to the chronicler, that the Council of 1407 began, and Easter Sunday in that year fell on 27 March, so that the assumption that the crisis arose early in March cannot be very far wrong. The Treasurer of Calais was dismissed, as has been said, on 9 March. Then, on the 14th Lord Furnival, the Treasurer of England, died. Thus at the critical moment the Exchequer was left without a head, and the Archbishop was deprived of one of his senior colleagues. From 10 March until 3 April, the Exchequer was closed for the Easter vacation. When it re-opened on the following day a further £5,000 from the fifteenth was paid in, and a few smaller receipts followed, but no money was paid out until after the appointment of the new Treasurer. This was Nicholas Bubwith, Bishop of London, who took office on 16 April.

Bubwith was one of the old type of clerical civil servants. A long career as a king's clerk had brought him through the offices of Master of the Rolls and Keeper of the Privy Seal to this final appointment of Treasurer. As a reward for his services he had been made Bishop of London, and was shortly to be translated to Salisbury and thence to Bath and Wells. Thus Bubwith brought a wealth of administrative experience to reinforce the Archbishop's statecraft.

Both were sorely needed, for by this time the Council was grappling with the financial problem. If the words "at London" are to be taken literally, the meetings were probably held, either in the Chapter House of the Black Friars, a favourite meeting place, or in one of the town houses, which most bishops and lay magnates possessed. Some of the meetings may well have been held in the royal palace at Westminster, close to the Exchequer, but the Black Friars would be a convenient place to meet the city merchants. The Archbishop, who was still at Lambeth, could be rowed in his barge to either place with almost equal ease. At all events, the negotiations with the merchants seem to have been concluded during the month of April, for on the 29th and 30th two royal grants announced that Richard Whittington, and other merchants of the staple, had lent the King £4,000 and promised that they should have full repayment from the first monies collected on the wool subsidies in certain ports. The second grant on the following day described the losses suffered by the merchants owing to the seizure of their wool, "the great substance of the wealth of our realm of England", by the soldiers at Calais. As a partial compensation the merchants were allowed to postpone payment of some of the export duties which they owed.

In making these loans Richard Whittington was the natural leader of the merchants, for he was at the time not only Mayor of London, his second term of office, but also Mayor of the Staple at Calais, and with the possible exception of John Hende, the wealthiest citizen of London. In addition to his share in the £4,000, Whittington lent another £1,000 of his own. John Hende, his colleague or rival, to whom the Crown was already indebted, lent £2,500, in return for which he was promised the keeping of the cocket seal in the port of London. This was the seal used by the customs collectors to mark the sacks of wool on which duty had been paid, and the holder of it could ensure that his own debts were paid before the money collected was sent to the Exchequer. Two other London citizens contributed small loans of their own, and the Albertini of Florence, the great company of merchants exporting wool to Italy, lent £1,000 on condition that they were allowed to export free of subsidy until they had recovered that sum.

The English and alien merchants together thus lent nearly £8,000, but this was still far short of the arrears due to the garrison at Calais, which probably amounted to nearly £20,000. The revenue continued to come in steadily and the Exchequer was able to issue £7,000 during May for the current expenses of Calais, but the total revenue of the year was to prove one of the lowest of the reign, and there was no money to spare for the arrears. Indeed, at the end of its term in July the Exchequer found itself unable to pay the salaries of some of its own staff.

The council therefore had to look around for some more loans.

John Norbury, the wealthy squire who had been Henry IV's first treasurer, was persuaded to lend £2,000. The clerks of the Chancery between them lent 500 marks, to be repaid out of the profits of their office. The Earl of Westmorland made a further loan of £500, and finally three members of the Council, the Lords Roos and Burnell and the Bishop of Durham, together found 600 marks, that is £400. All in all this brought the total up to £12,000. These sums were entered on the receipt roll of the Exchequer on 12 June, and paid out to the new Treasurer of Calais on the same day. Meanwhile, at the end of May, Sir John Tiptoft, now Treasurer of the King's household, was ordered to supervise the spending of the loans. By this time the nine weeks from Easter were over, and the main business of the Council was done. Only a few orders remained to be issued.

On 30 June the collectors of customs were officially informed of the loans, and of the arrangements for collecting and repaying the money. Half the wool subsidy was to be devoted to the payment of the current wages at Calais and the other half to the repayment of the debts, with the result that the King was left with no revenue at all from the subsidy for any other purpose. The instruction went on to prove the accuracy of the chronicler's report, by explaining that bonds guaranteeing the repayment of the loans had been sealed by the Archbishop of Canterbury, the Bishops of London, Winchester and Durham, the Duke of York, the Earl of Somerset, the Lords Grey, Burnell and Roos, Sir John Stanley, the Steward and John

Prophet, the Keeper of the Privy Seal. That is, by every member of the Council who had been named in Parliament on the preceding 22 December, except Lord Furnival, who had died, and the treasurer of the royal household, who had given up his office. This remarkable continuity of personnel shows that the arrangements made in Parliament were being carefully observed, and that the members of the Council were assuming a collective responsibility.

The full list may also explain the word "great" used both by the chronicler and in the official letters issued by the Chancery to describe this Council. When lists of the Council were issued it was generally implied that only a proportion of them would be in attendance at any one time. A full meeting, such as this one evidently was, would be sufficiently unusual to merit the word "great". But the expression "great Council" is generally taken to mean a still larger gathering, a meeting of magnates which was something between an ordinary Council and a full Parliament. On this occasion it may be supposed that John Norbury, a former Councillor, and the Earl of Westmorland, both of whom lent large sums, had been called into consultation. Richard Whittington and John Hende may also have attended in the role of councillors, as well as in that of lenders, and if these persons attended there may well have been others. For example, Sir John Tiptoft, who had been Speaker of the last Parliament and was now Treasurer of the royal household, was a likely member. But evidence is lacking.

The loans made it possible to postpone but not avoid the summoning of a new Parliament. In fact, the

postponement was a short one. On 20 October the Archbishop was busy explaining to a new Parliament which
had just met at Gloucester how the Councillors had
pledged themselves for the repayment of the loans which
they had raised. This Parliament, meeting away from the
independent and wealthy city of London, proved less
hostile to the King's government, and before it was dissolved on 2 December it had granted one and a half
fifteenths to help the Exchequer pay its way. Thanks to
Archbishop Arundel and his colleagues, Henry IV had
survived his worst financial crisis.

The pay of the garrison at Calais continued constantly
in arrears, but never quite so badly as in 1407. Indeed, it
was nearly fifty years before the shortage of money again
goaded the soldiers into such forceful measures as the
seizure of the wool. Henry V, in spite of the vast cost of the
armies with which he invaded France, made sure that
some £18,000 a year was provided for Calais. His first
objective was the conquest of Normandy, and therefore
Calais did not serve as his immediate base, but it was none
the less of great importance to him. It was in attempting
to reach Calais that he won his victory at Agincourt; and
once his conquests had begun to take shape, the road to
Calais became one of his main lines of communication.
He himself passed through Calais on his last journey to
and from England in 1421; and after his death in 1422 his
body was taken home by the same route. Under his son,
Henry VI, the provinces which he had conquered were
slowly lost, and by 1450 Calais was once more the only
English possession in the north of France. The English
export trade in wool was declining, as more of the wool

was made into cloth at home, but the Company of Merchants of the Staple was still a rich and powerful body. In 1454
the events of 1407 were repeated, the soldiers seized and
sold the wool in order to recover their arrears of pay.
Again the Government had to borrow heavily from the
merchants, and finally handed over to them the responsibility for paying the garrison. Henceforth the merchants
collected the subsidy on their own wool, paid for the
garrison, and accounted for any surplus at the Exchequer.
This arrangement was the final stage in the linking of the
pay of the garrison with the wool subsidy. In the Wars of
the Roses, Calais played an important part, serving as a
stronghold of Richard Neville, Earl of Warwick, the king-
maker, who amongst his many offices held that of Captain
of Calais. After that Edward IV in 1475, Henry VII in 1492,
and Henry VIII in 1513 and 1544, all used Calais as a base
for their invasions of France, but none of these expeditions
was pushed forward with great vigour or serious purpose,
apart from diplomatic and financial advantages. The
dream of conquering France was being slowly allowed to
fade. Under Henry VIII expenditure on the garrison was
slightly reduced, and the local revenues increased so that
the financial situation was easier. From 1542 Calais sent one
member to represent it in the English Parliament at Westminster, thus apparently achieving complete assimilation
as an English town: but the member was usually a royal
official, and the Englishness was more apparent than real.
The end was at hand. Early in 1558 Calais was overrun.
More than a thousand pieces of artillery fell into the hands
of the enemy. Queen Mary, who is best remembered as the
loser of Calais and the burner of her subjects, had no

forces to use for its recovery, and her husband, Philip of Spain, cared nothing for English possessions. Calais became a French town, and one more survival of the Middle Ages was swept away.

Jonathan Blow

NIBLEY GREEN 1470
The Last Private Battle Fought in England[1]

Hatred of her cousins, the Berkeleys of Berkeley Castle, dominated the entire active life of Margaret, wife and, later, widow of John Talbot, first Earl of Shrewsbury, the "English Achilles" and formidable opponent of Jeanne d'Arc. Her one object was to strip the Berkeleys of their vast inheritance—their lush manors which filled the whole Vale of Berkeley from the sea wall, built by their men-at-arms along the Severn's southern shore, to where the long western escarpment of the Cotswolds rises suddenly out of the plain: an immense estate which in places spilled over on to the brown, windswept tableland above. One and a half miles inland from the Severn, upon a knoll that commands a wide expanse of flat and sometimes flooded meadows, stands the squat bulk of the strongest fortress in the West of England, the castle from which the Berkeleys

[1] [Copyright © Jonathan Blow. Originally published in *History Today*, 11 (1962), pp. 598-610, and reprinted in P. Quennell, *Diversions of History*, London 1954. The battle was fought on 20 Mar. 1469/70, and this was mistakenly modernised as 1469 in the original article. The genealogical table on p. 111 provides many of the dates alluded to in the text as well as clarifying relationships.]

take their name, built of rose-red stone ferried across
the treacherous river from the crags of the Forest of Dean.
In its lofty hall—more than eleven yards high—the lords
of Berkeley at this time fed a private army of some three
hundred retainers. Bullocks by the score were fattened on
oats at their manor of Symondshall; flocks of tame pheas-
ants were fed on wheat at Berkeley. Three deer parks, of
which only one survives, lay within a few bow shots of the
ramparts; and four miles to the south-east stands Michael
Wood, then a tract of primaeval forest, much larger than
it is today and teeming with every sort of game. On the
mile-wide Severn, Thursday's tides were "the lord's
tides" and on that day all fish caught, or hunted down
among the shoals at low water—salmon and their at-
tendant lampreys, sole ("our Seaverne capon") and even
the giant sturgeon—were carried to the castle to feed the
host on Fridays.

In addition to their lands in Gloucestershire, the Berke-
leys held some thirty manors dotted throughout the Home
Counties and West Country, as well as properties in
Bristol and the City of London; and, to win this prize,
Margaret of Shrewsbury was ready to use any weapons,
from packed juries in the King's courts to the daggers of
hired assassins. Margaret was the daughter of Elizabeth,
the only child of Thomas, tenth Lord of Berkeley—
"Thomas the Magnificent"—favourite of the usurper
Bolingbroke, who made him guardian of the Welsh
Marches and Admiral of the King's fleet "west and south-
ward from the mouth of Thames". No earlier Berkeley
had ever kept such dazzling state. His sumptuous barge
was the marvel of the West. By a special and somewhat

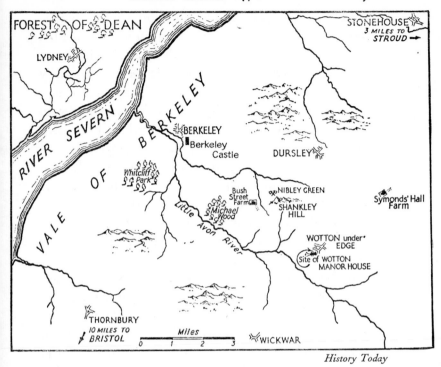

The Vale of Berkeley and Nibley Green.

costly Papal Bull, he was allowed a portable altar and the right to choose a "discreet priest", who was granted full powers to absolve him and his lady of all sins, including even those about which the Apostolic See must normally be first consulted[2]. At Berkeley and at his spacious manor house at Wotton-under-Edge, his stables were filled with the barrel-chested battle chargers, and lighter horses bred to gallop after hawk and hound, whose large eyes, tapering legs and delicate tracery of veins betrayed their Eastern ancestry. As wealth and power increased, he began to style himself in correspondence "We Thomas, lord of Berkeley . . . dated in our manor of Portbury" and the like, "which", says his chronicler, "none of his ancestors had so pompously before used to do"[3].

Riches he amassed by a striking variety of means—from teaching his shepherds to shear even the tails and buttocks of their charges, to piracy upon the high seas, once using his position as Admiral to "violently set upon and capture", off Bordeaux, a Genoese merchantman bound for London under the royal warrant of his sovereign with a cargo of wine worth £10,000. This was too much for Henry IV to stomach; and Thomas was ordered to restore the cargo or appear before his fellow Privy Coun-

[2] [Special and costly as they were, these were standard privileges granted by the Papacy to those willing to pay for them. Thomas's father had obtained similar concessions in his day.]

[3] [The writer from whom this and many of the other quotations in this article are taken is John Smyth, *Lives of the Berkeleys . . . and Description of the Hundred of Berkeley*, ed. Sir J. Maclean, in Transactions of the Bristol and Gloucestershire Archaeological Society, 3 vols., 1883-5. Smyth was Steward of the Lords of Berkeley in the reigns of Elizabeth I and James I, and the oral tradition of his day still preserved first-hand accounts of the battle at Nibley Green.]

sellors. "The sequel whereof", says the chronicler, "was
that the servants of this lord made restitution for part, but
went away with a great part of the rest of the Genoa
goods." War Thomas Berkeley usually made lucrative. As
Admiral he was entitled to three-quarters of the spoils of
naval actions. In 1405 a force of French knights, men-at-
arms, and cross-bowmen under the Marshal Jean de
Rieux landed on the Pembrokeshire coast to aid the
Welsh Prince Owen Glendower in his struggle against the
English. Thomas Berkeley at once put to sea, caught the
French fleet off Milford Haven, sank or burned fifteen of
their ships and captured the remaining fourteen "stuffed
with men, munition and victuals and so returned with
honour and profit". At Agincourt he was less successful.
He himself had failed to take a prisoner, but at twilight,
riding over the sodden ploughland, he caught sight of
Louis, Duke of Bourbon, in the hands of a common
English soldier. Much to the relief of the great French
nobleman, Thomas Berkeley told the soldier that he
would himself take charge of the prisoner; at which the
soldier—furious at being baulked of so rich a ransom—
drew his dagger and stabbed the Duke.

By marriage and skilful handling of his father-in-law,
Warin[4], Lord de Lisle, Thomas had also added to his
fortune no less than twenty-two manors scattered through
southern England from Northampton to Penzance. His
little bride, aged barely seven, he owed to his father
Maurice, a partial invalid since the sword-thrust he had

[4] [In the original article Gerard de Insula, son of Warin de Lisle, was
said to be Lord Berkeley's father-in-law. He was, in fact, his brother-in-
law, cp. G. E. C., *The Complete Peerage*, VIII (London 1932), pp. 51-3.]

received at Poitiers, who almost on his death-bed had negotiated the princely dowry of eleven hundred pounds. Maurice, feeling death close upon him, insisted on immediate marriage. So Thomas, then fourteen, was sent to the ceremony in Buckinghamshire clad in scarlet satin with an escort of three knights "furred with miniver" and twenty squires; while Maurice spent the wedding day in bed at Berkeley Castle, dressed in cloth of gold. Eleven hundred pounds was a fine dowry. But Thomas, succeeding at fifteen to the barony, "wittily" set himself "to fit the humours of the good old lord" his father-in-law, keeping open house for him at Berkeley Castle "at all hours", plying him with free fishing and hunting, quartering his arms and becoming his "unseparable companion". So the young Lord of Berkeley was not unduly surprised when his father-in-law—to the disgust of his male relatives —left to his daughter, the infant lady of Berkeley, every one of his twenty-two manors. But it was civil war that raised the power of Thomas Berkeley to the highest pinnacle in all his house's history. Richard II he had once sumptuously feasted in the great hall of his castle. Six years later—in 1393, the year of the quarrel between Arundel and John of Gaunt—"to avoid the danger of Court stormes, which then began to bluster with an hollow wind", Thomas obtained leave to tour the Continent, getting the King's written licence to take with him fifteen servants and the not ungenerous "travel allowance" of one thousand marks in money. Back once more at Berkeley, Thomas watched in silent apprehension the despotic rule of Richard and his upstart "Dukeling" favourites. When Bolingbroke was unjustly banished and Richard

and his favourites fastened on his vast estates, Lord
Berkeley's sympathies and secret correspondence went out
to the exiled Duke. At Berkeley, while King Richard was
in Ireland, the rebel army gathered "bloody with spurring,
fiery fed with haste" till all three courtyards and every
cranny of the castle were filled with the badge of Neville
and Percy. As Richard's uncle York approached with the
reluctant royalist levies, the ranks behind him melted and
came over to the rebels, followed by their old and incompetent commander. So it was from the lectern of
Berkeley church that Bolingbroke harangued the barons
of England. And it was Thomas Berkeley who was chosen
by that baronage to witness on their behalf King Richard's
renunciation of the Crown, first in Flint castle and later
in the Tower. Thomas never wavered in his support of
Bolingbroke. And Bolingbroke, as Henry IV, relied much
upon his many talents, choosing him as one of his Privy
Council and giving him great commands on sea and land.

Thus the Berkeley acres broadened; and Thomas made
money even out of the problem of his own successor. His
wife, whom he adored, died when she was thirty, leaving
him an only child, Elizabeth: but, though barely thirty-
eight and in full vigour, he refused always to remarry. No
one, while he lived, was allowed to see his written will.
When over fifty he sent for James Berkeley, his brother's
son, and brought him up as if he was his own. But he let
it be known to the mighty Earl of Warwick—then in
search of a bride for his eldest son—that Elizabeth was in
fact his sole heiress. Warwick leapt at so sumptuous a
prize, and the marriage allied Thomas very profitably to
one of the most powerful families in all England. But, to a

wealthy knight with a marriageable daughter, Thomas
confided that James was his real heir. Again the bait was
irresistible, and Thomas added to his coffers a dowry of
six hundred pounds. Still guarding his secret, Thomas the
Magnificent died, peacefully but suddenly, at Wotton in
1417. His nephew James, then twenty-three, was away
in Dorset. But Elizabeth and her husband, now Earl of
Warwick, were at his death bed and at once began a
feverish search through his many chests of deeds. At last
the will was found and unrolled. Considering Thomas's
immense possessions, it was not a very comprehensive
document. To Elizabeth his daughter he left his "best pair
of morninge mittens" and a tankard with twenty pounds in
it. And to James he left his best bed, his great jet tankard
and twenty suits of armour. Of his forty-two manors, his
city properties, his castle at Berkeley, and his great manor
house at Wotton there was no word.

Warwick, however, had two considerable advantages.
He was on the spot, and he was one of the foremost
captains and most trusted confidants of the new King,
Henry V. Seizing the title deeds, he set his clerks to copy-
ing the manorial rolls. And, sending couriers post haste
to the King, he secured within a week of Thomas's death
a royal warrant appointing him custodian of Berkeley
Castle. James, undaunted, issued a writ from Dorset and
"twelve of the most worshipfull gentlemen and of the best
liveliode within the County of Gloucester" were sworn
in as a jury. Warwick, "tasting the intention of the jury to
find against him", did all he could to stop the case, meanwhile holding manorial courts in all the Berkeley manors
and, armed with the title deeds, pocketing the rents. But,

while he was across the Channel aiding the King to
conquer Normandy, the jury reached a verdict. James was
to inherit Berkeley Castle and all the lands in Gloucestershire, a total of twelve manors. The rest, except Portbury
in Somerset, were to go to the Countess of Warwick. To
uphold the verdict was another matter. Warwick, through
his power at court, secured a privy seal forbidding James
to sue him, and then, marching on Berkeley with a great
host of retainers, besieged James in the castle. Many had
been "hurt and maymed, and some slayne" when the
mitred figure of the Bishop of Worcester rode up, and
secured an armistice.

James Berkeley, recognising he "was as a weak hopp . . .
having no strong pole to wind about", now "wisely
winneth with his purse the assistance of Humphrey, Duke
of Gloucester, the King's brother". In return for the huge
sum of a thousand pounds in cash and the large Welsh
estate of James's mother, worth four hundred pounds a
year, the royal Duke undertook to secure for James "the
quiet possession of the castle and lordship of Berkeley".
So at Windsor Castle, in the presence of their new
eleven-month-old sovereign Henry VI and the Regent,
the Duke of Gloucester, James was acknowledged
eleventh Lord of Berkeley and reconciled with Warwick,
both binding themselves to submit to the judgment of the
Lord Chief Justice[5] and the Bishop of Worcester the
question of the Berkeley lands in Gloucestershire and the
quarrels of their retainers, "excepting those that arose

[5] [There was no single Lord Chief Justice at this date: but the Chief
Justice of the Common Bench and the Chief Justice of the King's Bench
were both among the arbitrators appointed.]

between their servants at Hammersmyth by London, and of the blows then given, which they have submitted to the Duke of Gloucester". James was not pleased with the judgement, given three years later, by the Bishop and Chief Justice. Of the twelve Gloucestershire manors three were then awarded to the Warwicks; three manors which were to become the Alsace-Lorraine of the mortal struggle now ahead—Wotton, with its splendid manor house, guarding the foot of the pass that winds up from the Severn Valley on to the heights above; Symondshall on the edge of the table land; and Cowley, with its great flocks of sheep, an isolated outpost far away across the rolling uplands near the first springs of the Thames. Yet so long as Warwick lived, James accepted this unfavourable judgment. He could not well do otherwise, for at the Windsor reconciliation both litigants had pledged themselves to pay a thousand marks if they broke the verdict of the arbitrators; and the Berkeley treasury, shorn of three-quarters of its rents, had been drained almost dry by bribes and litigation. The eleventh Lord of Berkeley was forced even to pawn the chalices and copes of the castle chapel.

After thirteen years of parsimonious peace, news came from France that the great Earl was dead; and at once the Berkeleys seized the three disputed manors. Warwick had left no son; but his eldest daughter, Margaret, had become the second wife of his fellow general John Talbot, Earl of Shrewsbury; and Margaret was to prove the most ruthless of all the Berkeley's foes. Of her two younger sisters, one had married Edmund Beaufort, Duke of Somerset, the powerful favourite of the Queen, and the other a younger son of the great house of Neville. Such was the coalition, holding the greatest offices the Crown could give and virtually controlling the simple, brittle-minded King, that now faced the impoverished Lord of Berkeley. A Warrant, bearing the great seal of England, arrived at Gloucester, "turning him out of the Commission of the peace, of subsedy and all other commissions that 'gave him' any command, lustre or authority in his country". James was imprisoned in the Tower. Released on the ruinous bail of one thousand pounds, he was ordered to appear, when summoned, in person before the King in chancery. But—considering the unequal standing of the litigants—the King's judges proved remarkably fair. Margaret and her sisters were awarded the three disputed manors, which their mother and father had held for thirteen years, but James was awarded the castle and remaining nine manors of the Gloucestershire estate. And when John Talbot, on sailing for France, asked Parliament for protection for one year from all suites of law, it was granted only on condition that neither the three sisters nor their husbands entered James's manors. James, however, defied the decision of the judges, and absolutely refused to give up three manors. When a Talbot herald served him at Wotton Manor with a summons to appear in court, James and his retainers forced the herald to chew up and swallow the summons—wax seal, parchment and all.

Now it was open war. Both sides—Talbot and Berkeley—tried by night to collect the rents from each other's luckless tenants. From the impregnable refuge of Berkeley Castle, William—James's eldest son—led raids northwards up the Severn Valley to plunder the Talbot manors

of Whaddon, just short of Gloucester, and wealthy
Painswick on the hills above. Margaret's son, John
Talbot, lately created Viscount Lisle, fired the town of
Berkeley beneath the castle walls; while the Berkeleys, not
daring to sally out, cursed him from the ramparts. Since
it was impossible for James, directing raid and counter-
raid, to leave the scene of action, his wife, the saintly lady
Isabel, who had journeyed to London to plead his case in
the King's courts, wrote to give him warning: "Revered
lord and husband, I commend me to you with all my
heart, desiring always to hear of your good wellfare,
which God maintayne. And it please you to heare how I
fare, Roger and Jacket (the Talbot lawyers) have asked
surety of peace for mee, for their intent was to bringe mee
into the Tower. But I trust in God tomorrow that I shall
goe bayle unto the next Term, and soe goe home, and then
to come againe. . . . Bee well ware of false counsell. Keep
well your place. The Earl of Shrewsbury lyeth right nye
you, and shapeth all the wyles hee can to distresse you and
yours. . . . For he saith he will never come to the King
againe till hee have done you an ill turne. Sur your matter
speedeth and doth right well, save my daughter costeth
great goods. At the reverence of God send money, or else
I must lay my horse to pledge and come home on my feet.
Keep well all about you till I come home, and trete not
without mee. Then all thinges shall be well with the grace
of Almighty God, who have you in his keeping. Written
at London the Wednesday after Whitsun. Your wife the
lady of Berkeley."

James borrowed twenty-two marks by pawning a gilt
mass book, a chest of red satin stoles, two altar cloths, and

a massive silver chalice; and every night he slept with the
castle keys beneath his pillow. News now reached the
castle that a sizeable sum of recently collected Talbot rents
was in temporary storage about ten miles from Berkeley,
at the house of one Richard Andrews. At nightfall, William
sent out a raiding party of twenty mounted retainers under
a squire called Rice Tewe. But, as they rode out of the
castle and headed eastward for the hills, some hidden eyes
had seen them pass, and word was galloped to Wotton
Manor, where the Talbots were now installed. Rice Tewe
reached and surrounded the house of the unsuspecting
Andrews, burst in and "upturned every corner", without,
however, finding the gold. Stoking the fire, he thrust into
it a branding iron "till it was glowing hott", and promised
to seat Andrews upon it if he would not show them the
money. This threat was enough, and rapid digging beneath
the floor revealed a chest well filled with golden sovereigns.
They hurried it out to their horses, to find themselves surrounded by Talbot men-at-arms under Viscount Lisle. A
sharp sword fight followed and, after a most spirited
resistance, Tewe and his surviving comrades were
secured. Lord Lisle had a few private words with Tewe.
The prisoners were then fastened to their own horses and
placed in the middle of the Talbot troop, which made
rapidly for Berkeley. As they reached the sleeping town,
the sky above the high escarpment behind them to the
east had already begun to lighten: but it was still too dark
to distinguish clearly the badges worn by the retainers.
Now above them rose the Castle itself. Tewe—with a
dagger at his back—hailed the watch; and there was a
pause while a yeoman of James Berkeley's chamber was

sent to ask his master for the keys. At length the draw-bridge was lowered and the portcullis raised.

Roused from their beds by Talbot sword points, James Berkeley and his four sons were held prisoners in their rooms. Soon, in the courtyard below, they heard the rasping stick and the voice of Margaret. Exactly what happened at the castle, during the next eight weeks, we do not know: but James and his sons signed some remark-able agreements. Herein they stated that, "without any dures, constraint or coartion" by the Earl and Countess, they had considered among themselves their "great ryots and tresspasses . . . and other divers abhominable deeds which they had done to the said Earl, Countess and Vis-count . . . with the great number of right rioutous and evill disposed people" they had kept within the castle during their "mischeevous rule". And, "considering the great and huge costs which they had put the Earl and Countess too . . . and also the great punition which they had deserved after due course of the lawe, likely upon them to ensue and fall . . . they freely offered to the Earl and Countess" a thousand pounds and two hundred pounds to Viscount Lisle. They renounced all claim to the three dis-puted manors, and would remain Margaret's "true cozens, faithfull men and servants". And they would lease to her their castle, retaining in it only "housroome for them-selves and six servants"—a clause cunningly inserted by Margaret to mask from the outside world that they were prisoners in their own fortress. These agreements signed, James and his four sons were placed in the midst of a great rout of Talbot retainers and carried down to Bristol, where the Mayor was sent for; and before him they were made to acknowledge the agreements, and pledged themselves to pay £10,000, if any were not carried out in full. Bundled back to Berkeley, they were next taken before a Judge Bingham at Cirencester, where a jury, gathered from the remotest parts of the country, gave judgment for the Talbots. When Isabel, James's wife, who was still at large, appeared at a court at Gloucester on her imprisoned Lord's behalf, Margaret had her thrown into Gloucester castle. There she mysteriously died—a deed which so shocked a servant of one of Margaret's accomplices that, the same night, he stabbed his master.

Meanwhile, secret and urgent appeals were reaching London from the nobles and bourgeoisie of Gascony, which the Queen and Privy Council—distracted by the first mutterings of civil war in England—had allowed the King of France to over-run. The Gascons begged for Talbot; and the ageing Achilles set sail for France. With him, Margaret sent James Berkeley's two youngest sons, James and Thomas. Bordeaux opened its gates with enthusiasm to the little English army; and, a few weeks later, Lord Lisle went out to reinforce his father, leaving Margaret alone at Berkeley to guard the three remaining prisoners. Without his wife, James was no match for Margaret; and she had induced him to issue a writ to test the Cirencester judgment—whereupon her friend James Clifford, Sheriff of Gloucestershire, declared the Bristol pledges broken and the entire estate forfeit to Margaret to meet the agreed penalty of £10,000—when suddenly all private passions froze at the fearful news from France. Shrewsbury had led a furious attack upon the spiked ditch and high stockade of the French camp before Castillon;

the French cannon had ploughed through the advancing
column, and a ball had shattered Shrewsbury's leg. Then,
as the French closed round in overwhelming numbers,
Lisle had stood at bay over his wounded father. All trapped
together in a tightening circle, Thomas Berkeley had been
taken and James Berkeley slain; and Margaret's son and
husband, undaunted by the odds and refusing quarter,
had side by side been killed.

For a short time there was peace in Gloucestershire; but,
although Margaret was at first half stunned, the presence
of her little grandson Thomas, now Viscount Lisle, soon
revived all her calculated cunning in schemes for his
advancement. James, on the other hand, at sixty-three, now
executed a masterly stroke of policy by marrying Joan
Talbot, the late Earl's daughter by his first countess and a
sister of the new Earl—a triumph which he owed largely
to the new Earl's distaste for his step-mother, Margaret.
The odds were becoming altogether more even. The great
seal of England, which Margaret's sister's husband, the
Duke of Somerset, had used against the luckless James,
was now in other and more neutral hands. The White
Rose was now threatening the Red; and Somerset fell in
the first street-scuffle at St Albans. Marriage to Joan Talbot
paid James immediate dividends—his liberty, his castle,
and the nine Gloucestershire manors which none of the
innumerable courts and arbitrations had ever failed to
grant him. And it deprived Margaret of the support of the
great Shrewsbury Earldom. With what dignity she could,
she retreated to the manor-house at Wotton, taking with
her her grandson Thomas, Viscount Lisle, an impetuous
and attractive youth with all his grandsire's fiery courage

and a passionate desire to emulate the deeds of knight errantry. By Margaret, Thomas was brought up to hate his Berkeley cousins as the Infidel or Anti-Christ, as men who had robbed him of his birthright. But for the moment she did not feel strong enough to launch a fresh offensive.

Supported by Joan Talbot, James now had every chance to win back Wotton, Symondshall and Cowley. But, a tired and sad old man, he was utterly weary of the struggle that had blighted his entire life since the age of twenty-three; and, to the disgust of his heir William, he signed a pact with Margaret for the rest of their joint lives. William, however, succeeding at thirty-eight in 1463, was a far more able and ambitious foe. Nine manors were not enough to give the Lords of Berkeley the power and wealth to which they were accustomed. Prudently securing his step-mother Joan's support, with a handsome annual settlement, he at once petitioned the new-crowned Yorkist King for the three disputed manors. Edward IV sent the petition to the Lord Chancellor, who referred it to the courts. William wisely took the precaution, while in London for the hearing, of living in sanctuary at Westminster Abbey[6]; and the long-drawn proceedings suddenly flared up when he accused Margaret of trying to have him murdered. One Chamberlen, a sanctuary man of Westminster, revealed to William that he had been offered by Margaret a handsome sum to accompany him, when next he journeyed back to

[6] [On the frequently used and abused rights of sanctuary, see J. J. Jusserand, *English Wayfaring Life in the Middle Ages*, 3rd ed., New York 1931, pp. 157 ff. Edward IV's Queen, Elizabeth Woodville, took sanctuary in Westminster when Richard III seized the throne in 1483, accompanied by her daughters and Richard, Duke of York. She was prevailed upon to release the young Richard to her enemies.]

Berkeley, and murder him on the road. Some Berkeley servants were then hidden in a secret place in the Abbey, from which they claimed to have overheard the offer urgently repeated by one of Margaret's servants. Margaret angrily denied the whole story as "too abhomonable for a Christian creature to have done" and a product of William's "sinfull imagination"; but, before the witnesses could be examined, she died in the summer of 1468—a "yeare of jubile to this lord William, for in it death rid him of three great lady widowes . . . Countess Margaret, Duchess Alienor of Somerset (her sister) and Viscountess Jone", widow of Margaret's only son.

Courts of law were not to the taste of Thomas Talbot, second Viscount Lisle, who at the age of nineteen was now left with his young bride Margaret Herbert, daughter of the Earl of Pembroke, to carry out the last "angry charge and motherly command" of Margaret, who, besides the three manors and various rights of fishing, had bequeathed him a plan of action on which for some time she had been stealthily at work. Berkeley Castle, for a force as small as Thomas Talbot's, was virtually impregnable. But Thomas's father had found means of entry other than by direct assault. Holt, William's keeper of Whitcliff Park, the great deer park that survives today a half mile from the castle, now began to receive by night a secret visitor— Robert Vele, Lord Lisle's engineer. And there fell into William's hands a letter—still among the Berkeley papers —from Holt to Maurice Kinge, the porter of the castle gates, reminding him of conversations they had had when they "lay together at Micheldene in one bed" and "in the Chapple out of the great chamber" at Berkeley; and asking

Kinge to "geve very faythfull credence unto Mr Robert
Vele," since the "purposes" of which they had "com-
muned" were "now . . . brought to the poynt". Kinge's
share in "the matter" would be an annuity and the post of
keeper at Wotton deer park. His letter having been discovered, Holt fled to Wotton Manor House: but con-
fessions were extracted from Maurice Kinge which revealed a plot to open by night the castle gates to Thomas
Talbot.

Baulked of this plan, Thomas now taunted William to
come out of his great fortress and put their quarrel to the
test, either of single combat or of a pitched battle in the
open between their private armies. A Talbot herald rode
down to Berkeley with a written challenge: "William,
called Lord Berkeley. I marveill ye come not forth with
all your carts of gunnes, bowes, with oder ordinance, that
yet set forward to come to my manor of Wotton to bete
it down upon my hand. I let you wit ye shall not nede to
come soe nye. For I trust to God to mete you nere home
with Englishmen of my own nation and neighbours,
whereas ye by suttle craft have blown it about in diverse
places of England that I should intend to bring in Welsh-
men for to destroy and hurt my own nation and country.
I lete thee wit, I was never soe disposed, nere never will be.
And to the proof hereof, I require thee of knighthood and
of manhood to appoynt a day to meet me half way, there
to try between God and our two hands all our quarrell
and title of right, for to eschew the shedding of Christian
menns blood. Or els at the same day bringe the uttermost
of thy power, and I shall mete thee. An answere of this by
writinge, as ye will abide by, according to the honour and

H—E.S.G.

order of Knighthood—Thomas Talbot the Viscount
Lisle."

William answered the same day by return of herald—
19 March, 1470. Security was impossible while a descend-
ant of Margaret's lived. The three manors were a first step,
and Thomas a stumbling block, on the road to his great
personal ambitions. The moment was opportune; for
Edward IV was fully occupied with the rebellion of his
younger brother, "false, fleeting perjured Clarence", and
the great Earl of Warwick had turned against the King
whom he had made. As the twelfth Lord of Berkeley,
William goaded Thomas with the Talbot's recent ennoble-
ment and the proximity of Shrewsbury to the despised
land of Wales: "Thomas Talbot, otherwise called Viscount
Lisle, not longe continued in that name but a new found
thing brought out of Strange Contryes. I marveill greatly
at thy strange and lewd writing." But the prospect of single
combat with a fanatic, twenty years younger than himself,
did not appeal to the now middle-aged William; and he
told Thomas he knew "right well there is no such deter-
mination of land in this Relme used. And I ascertaine thee
that my livelode, as well my manor of Wotton as my
Castle of Berkeley, be entayled to me by fine record in the
king's Courts by the advice of all the Judges of this land
in that dayes being." Had single combat not been out of
date, however, William assured Thomas he would have
been delighted to accommodate him "in every poynt that
belongeth to a knight". But, "to ease" his adversary's
"malitious heart", he agreed to fight a pitched battle.
"Faile not tomorrow to be at Niblyes green at eight or
nyne of the clock which standeth in the borders of the

livelode that thou keepest untruly from me . . . And the trouth shall be shewed by the marcy of God." He added that, far from bringing his uttermost power, he would "not bring the tenth part that" he could "make"—and then sent couriers hurtling south to Bristol to get help from its merchants, and west across the mile wide Severn to raise the foresters of Dean.

Maurice Berkeley—the eldest of William's younger brothers—was in bed at Thornbury when the urgent appeal arrived in the middle of the night, and "stole from his young wife" to ride north for the muster with all the men he could. From Bristol came his father-in-law, the merchant Philip Mead, with a fellow alderman and a band of armed servants. William's tenants and paid men-at-arms had, meanwhile, been reinforced by a number of miners and foresters from the far side of the Severn, among them Black Will, a colossus of a man and an archer of high repute. Mounting their battle chargers, the Lord of Berkeley and his other brother, Thomas, now led this force out into the night. They rode along the Little Avon, its still surface shattered every few hundred yards by noisy little cataracts, and plunged into the primaeval depths of Michael Wood, picking their way through the giant oaks, beneath which the hounds of Thomas the Magnificent had so often hunted deer. Its eastern outskirts then stretched a good mile nearer to the Cotswolds than they do today; and in those outskirts—close to the present site of Bush Street Farm—Lord Berkeley halted. There he was joined by Maurice and the Bristol aldermen, raising their numbers to over a thousand men; and there they lay, concealing their great strength. Before them, soon outlined by the dawn, rose the long escarpment of the Cotswolds, rising on their left to Drakestone's Point, while on the right two precipitous and clean-cut spurs stuck out into the misty valley—Westridge Wood and Wotton Hill. But, a few yards immediately in front of where the Berkeleys lay, stands a rounded foothill, blotting out a length of the escarpment behind—Shankley Hill, its comfortable slopes still striped with the boundary marks of the manorial field system, with the square tower of Nibley Church, then newly built, looking over its northern shoulder. Ten o'clock had passed, when the skyline beside Nibley Church was broken by Talbot pennants. Over the crest and down the slopes came the armoured horsemen and the dismounted Talbot tenantry—followed by a mob of small boys who swarmed up into trees to watch the fight.

William noted with satisfaction that Thomas was out-numbered. And then his archers let fly together, the horns sounded and the whole Berkeley army burst out into the open. Of the details of this battle—the last ever fought in England between two private armies—we know little. That casualties were considerable we have learned from the excavation in Victorian times of the large communal grave by Nibley Church, in which a hundred and fifty skeletons were found. We know that, for an instant, Lord Lisle raised his visor, and that, at that moment, he reeled from his saddle with Black Will's arrow in his cheek—to be stabbed to death as he lay helpless. His young wife, who was pregnant, was waiting at Wotton Manor House for news of the fight, when suddenly, round Wotton Church and through the churchyard, surged a confused flood of

Talbot retainers with the Berkeley's hard on their heels. William rushed the gates of the great manor-house, and ransacked it for the deeds and the manorial rolls that Thomas's great-grandparents, the Warwicks, had seized at the death of Thomas the Magnificent. The whole house was in uproar. The deeds were found and William returned triumphantly to Berkeley carrying with him the Lisle arms, ripped down from the wall, the roof-lead and the ovens— the latest fifteenth-century pattern—still preserved at Berkeley Castle.

Victory was complete; for, sixteen days after Lord Lisle was slain and Wotton plundered, his widow had a miscarriage. "Thus", says the chronicler, "did all the sons joyne in revenge of the innocent bloud of that virtuous and princely lady Isabel their mother, malitiously spilt at Gloucester seaventeen yeares before by Margaret . . . for that blowe swept away all her issue male from off the earth". Lisle's widow and his sister, their relatives and their descendants, pursued the Berkeleys through the courts for 150 years. Not till the reign of James I was "the bloud spilt" at Nibley Green "clean dried up"; and a judge then remarked that successive Berkeley litigants had "beaten smooth the pavements betweene Temple barre and Westminster hall". Yet the savage feud that sprang from the facetious will of Thomas the Magnificent brought his family one tremendous benefit. It kept them so en-grossed in their own private war that they took almost no part in that mass suicide of the true baronage of England— the Wars of the Roses. Historic earldoms, such as those of Devonshire and Salisbury, which had carried great martial power and great obligations, passed into the hands of the middle-class officials of the Tudors, who sprouted like mushrooms from the loot of the monastery-lands. But the Berkeleys—direct descendants of the youngest of the brothers who fought at Nibley Green—still live in Berkeley Castle and hold the manors by the Severn, and their hounds today still hunt through Michael Wood and Whitcliff Park.

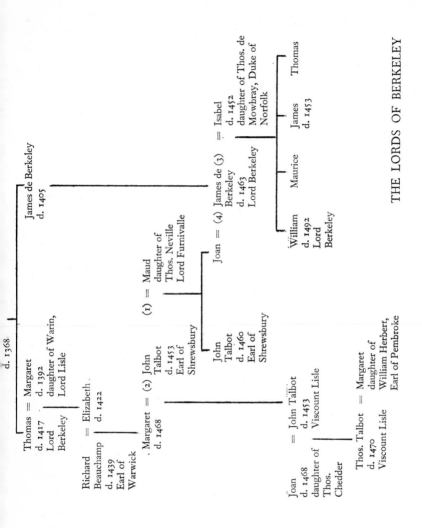

THE LORDS OF BERKELEY

A. R. Myers

THE CHARACTER OF RICHARD III[1]

"Shakespeare, the only history of England I ever read", the great Duke of Marlborough is said to have remarked; and Shakespeare's enormous influence in shaping subsequent concepts of fifteenth-century England is nowhere better illustrated than in the case of the character of Richard III. His picture is the more effective because it is so skilfully simple—the portrait of evil incarnate. Born a monster, before his time, hunchbacked, "not made to court an amorous looking-glass", Richard pretends loyalty to his father and his brother Edward only in order to further his own wicked ambitions. Under a cloak of virtue, he kills, one by one, those who stand between him and the throne, whether it is a defenceless boy after the battle of Tewkesbury, a saintly old king in the Tower, or his own brother in the same fortress a few years later. On the death of Edward IV, so the Shakespearian version runs, Richard cunningly allays suspicion by protesting obsequious loyalty to his nephew, Edward V, whom he nevertheless shuts up in the Tower with his younger brother. After

[1] [Copyright © A. R. Myers. Originally published in *History Today*, IV (1954), pp. 511-21.]

the beheading without trial of Rivers, Grey, Vaughan, and Hastings, Richard does not hesitate to have it publicly proclaimed that his nephews are bastards, and, in order to make Edward IV appear illegitimate, too, does not even stop at accusing his own mother of adultery. By this time we are well prepared for his seizure of the throne, his murders of his nephews and his wife, and his attempt to marry his niece. But the avenging angel soon appears in the person of the "virtuous and holy" Henry Tudor, to whom all decent men quickly flock. Deserted by nearly all, lamented by none, "the son of Hell" falls at Bosworth, slain by the man whom Heaven has sent to restore justice, unity, and prosperity to England.

Incredible as this portrait of a total villain may seem to our generation, conscious of the complexity of human psychology, it is not merely a dramatist's creation. It is true that Shakespeare was the contemporary of dramatists fascinated by the triumph and downfall of evil men: but even in quite small details Shakespeare can be shown to be drawing on what was to be found in history books. It does not, however, require much investigation to see that the historical material on which he relied is open to serious objections. It was produced under a powerful dynasty which stood to gain by the character of Richard III being painted as black as possible; for, if England was from 1483 to 1485 oppressed by a usurping tyrant, the invasion of Henry Tudor was not merely that of a landless adventurer with a weak claim to the throne, but that of the gracious deliverer appointed by Providence. It is not surprising that the improbable picture of Richard as a diabolical monster, whose courage was his sole redeeming feature, should have provoked a violent reaction as soon as the last Tudor monarch was laid to rest; and the fears of a disputed succession and civil war had died away. In Sir George Buc's biography[2], written between 1605 and 1621, we have the first substantial defence of Richard III—no half-hearted apology, but a vigorous rebuttal of every charge brought against him. This should logically have involved a condemnation of Henry VII; for if Richard III was not a usurper, then Henry was. Buc did argue that Perkin Warbeck was indeed one of the sons of Edward IV: but he also goes out of his way to say that he was not impugning the title of Henry VII, who is described as a wise and religious prince. This was prudent; for not only did James I claim the throne of England through a Tudor princess, but English people were already looking back on Elizabeth's reign as a golden age.

By the time of Horace Walpole, there was no need for tenderness towards the reputation of Henry VII if one wished to defend Richard III; and in his *Historic Doubts* Walpole not only cleared Richard of all the principal

[2] [Editions of this and of most of the other works cited in Dr Myers's review of the historiography of Richard III's reign can be identified conveniently in the bibliography for C. H. Williams's chapter "England: The Yorkist Kings, 1461-85", in *The Cambridge Medieval History*, VIII, London (1936), pp. 912-4, 919, 922-3. Editions not found there are Chronicle of Tewkesbury in C. L. Kingsford, *English Historical Literature in the Fifteenth Century*, Oxford (1913), pp. 376-8; *The Anglica Historia of Polydore Vergil*, ed. Denys Hay, (Camden Society, 3rd Series, LXXIV), London, 1950; *Hall's Chronicles containing the History of England*, London, 1809; Bernardus Andreas, *Historia Regis Henrici Septimi*, ed. J. Gairdner, London, 1858; *Grafton's Chronicle or History of England*, 2 vols., London, 1809; *Holinshed's Chronicles of England, Scotland and Ireland*, 6 vols., London, 1807-8, which includes John Stow, *The Chronicles of England*; *The Usurpation of Richard III*, ed. C. A. J. Armstrong, Oxford, 1936 (Dominic Mancini).]

accusations, but suggested that it was Henry VII who murdered the young King Edward V. Since then, other writers, in a more detailed study of the evidence than that made by either Buc or Walpole, have taken a favourable view of Richard III, until the most complete vindication on a serious level was reached with the biography of Sir Clements R. Markham, published in 1906. With the vehemence and forensic skill of a defending counsel, he argued that all the evidence against Richard is tainted, either because it was written by those who hated him, or because it was composed to please the Tudors, whose interest it was to besmirch his character. Everything that Tudor writers say against Richard is therefore suspect; everything that they say in his favour can be accepted all the more readily as it comes from his foes; and where the evidence is not clear (which is often) Markham was fond of using a "must have been" to resolve the doubt in Richard's favour. As a result, Richard stands forth, not as the villain of Tudor legend, but as a "gallant young hero" and almost a saint. He was, thought Markham, one of the best kings England has ever had, and his evil reputation is entirely due to "the accumulated garbage and filth of centuries of calumny". Not that Markham's book lacks its villain: but he turns out to be Henry VII. Cold, cunning, and merciless, an "adventurer who waded through the blood of innocent men to his usurped throne", he it was who murdered the princes in the Tower between 16 June and 6 July, 1486. He followed this up with the murder of other rivals, with the intimidation of his wife, and with the imprisonment of those who, like his mother-in-law, knew too much of his crimes; and he died, like the coward he was, "full of terrors, prematurely old and worn out", at the "early age" of fifty-two.

This is indeed a far cry from the Shakespearian Richard. What are we to believe when offered portraits of Richard which have scarcely anything in common except the name?

It must be acknowledged that Markham had some strong ground on which to build his case. First, there is the fact that there is not much strictly contemporary evidence for the character of Richard III; and it is possible to follow the growth of some stories against Richard which move further and further from such contemporary evidence as we have. For example, contemporary writers say nothing about the murder in cold blood of Edward of Lancaster by Richard and others after the battle of Tewkesbury. Perhaps in such a matter we can refuse to accept the silent smoothness of *The Arrivall of Edward IV*, an official Yorkist version intended as an apologia to foreign governments: but the same cannot be our reaction to a Lancastrian contemporary, John Warkworth, whose chronicle merely says: "And ther was slayne in the felde, Prynce Edward, which cryede for socoure to his brother-in-lawe, the Duke of Clarence". Warkworth's silence is the more remarkable because elsewhere he makes some adverse comments on the Yorkist leaders. A chronicle of Tewkesbury, in an account of the battle probably compiled soon afterwards, and in a spirit rather hostile to Edward IV, also merely states that Prince Edward was slain in the field. Moreover, the memoirs of Philippe de Comines say the same; and this is noteworthy, since he almost certainly derived his information from Lancastrian refugees in Burgundy, who would not have been loath to indict the Yorkist leaders if there had been any accusation to make. Yet in spite of this consensus of contemporary opinion, we find sixteenth-century writers gradually building up a detailed charge against Richard. First, two London chronicles, Fabyan's *Chronicle*, completed in 1504, and the *Great Chronicle*, finished in 1512, say that Prince Edward was brought before Edward IV and killed by the King's attendants for impertinence. Then Polydore Vergil, an Italian who began his *Anglica Historia* at the request of Henry VII but ended it only in the reign of his son, added to this by naming Gloucester among the murderers. The influential Edward Hall, a zealous supporter of Henry VIII, took over Vergil's account, and made it more vivid with further details. Later writers largely copied Hall, and so we reach the Shakespearian picture of a captive, but spirited youth, struck down by Edward IV for his courageous words; and stabbed to death by Gloucester and Clarence as he lies defenceless on the ground. In this there is an interesting resemblance to the growth of the legend of Suffolk's share in the "murder" of the "good Duke Humphrey" of Gloucester in 1447. We see the construction of a detailed certainty of crime on a foundation of rumour which first appears some twenty years after Richard's death, and over thirty years after the incident described.

There are other elements in the Tudor picture of Richard which rest on sources open to serious criticism. The first descriptions of Richard's person came in John Rous's *Historia Regum Angliae*, written between 1489 and 1491 and dedicated to Henry VII. Here we are first informed that Richard was weak of body, deformed, with the right shoulder higher than the left, born with hair and teeth after two years in his mother's womb. Born a monster, he was destined to become like the scorpion which was ascendant at his birth. In contrast to this is Henry VII, who is said to have had an angelic countenance that won the love of all who beheld it. Yet Rous, the old chantry priest who could write this, had only a few years earlier paid a fulsome tribute to Richard in which he stressed the King's legitimacy and praised his wise and virtuous rule.

With the *History of Henry VII* by Bernard André, an Austin friar whom Henry VII made royal historiographer and tutor to Prince Arthur, the legend took a long step forward. His account is not a history, but a portrait of two figures, the one of darkness, the other of light, black Richard and the angelic Richmond. And when we come to the *History of Richard III* written by Sir Thomas More about 1513, Richard now appears as evil incarnate. Nevertheless, this work cannot be simply rejected as solely the propaganda of Cardinal Morton. The case for More's authorship has been pretty conclusively proved, and it is unreasonable to do as Markham does and limit More's informants to Morton, who had been dead at least thirteen years. There were others who had taken part in public affairs while Richard was on the throne and were not only still alive when More wrote, but were his friends, acquaintances, or neighbours. But several of these persons, such as Bishop Fox or Christopher Urswick, were known opponents of Richard III, and others were burdened with a past which was better forgotten or modified in the reign of Henry VIII. In any case they were recalling events of between thirty and fifty years before; and there was little to be learnt of Richard III from books when More wrote. The short, but mostly excellent account of the Yorkist period by the continuator of the *Croyland Chronicle*, who had been a Councillor of Edward IV, was composed in 1486: but it was unknown in More's day and remained unprinted until 1684. Moreover, it is questionable whether More regarded himself as writing history; his story is much more like a drama, unfolded in magnificent prose, for which fidelity to historical fact is scarcely relevant. It is possible that he took up and intensified the current legends about the monster Richard as a means of launching a discreet attack on the unscrupulous policies of the rulers of his own day. We know that, like his friend Erasmus, More was much concerned about the vital necessity of truly Christian princes in that age of powerful monarchies; and, as a warning, he may have wished to present Richard as a personified Vice in a Renaissance equivalent of a morality play. Certainly, the serious errors of fact, and the blanks left in the manuscript for the insertion of various dates and names, seem to indicate that More never revised his *History of Richard III*, and did not intend it to be published as he left it. Yet it exercised enormous influence; it was embodied with only slight alterations in all subsequent chronicles of importance, such as those of Hall, Grafton, Holinshed, and Stow; and it formed the basis of much of Shakespeare's picture.

The history of Polydore Vergil, which was second only to More's biography in importance for shaping the Elizabethan view of Richard, makes a greater attempt at impartiality, and Polydore Vergil's picture of Richard is in various respects less hostile than that of More. Yet Polydore Vergil's work was much influenced by the fact that he had been called upon to produce an apologia for the House of Tudor and that it was necessary for an unpopular foreigner to be very circumspect to keep the favour of Henry VIII, a point recently brought out still more clearly by Professor Denys Hay's comparisons of the printed versions with the manuscripts. And as succeeding chroniclers used Polydore Vergil's history, bodily or as a basis, for those parts of the Yorkist reigns not touched upon by More, Vergil's accusations against Richard become very potent.

It is this peculiar characteristic of the sources for Richard's life—that all those which formed the Elizabethan picture of the King were written after his death under influences hostile to him—which somewhat mars Dr Gairdner's important biography (first published in 1878, and revised in 1898). Gairdner was a great scholar who did much by his learning to clarify the picture of Richard III and to discredit some of the more extreme charges made against him. Yet, Gairdner was by temperament and experience a conservative who revered tradition; and he recorded in the preface to his biography his view that "a minute study of the facts of Richard's life has tended more and more to convince me of the general fidelity of the portrait with which we have been made familiar by Shakespeare and Sir Thomas More". This result was reached because his "larger study of history in other periods" convinced him that the "attempt to discard tradition in the examination of original sources of history is, in fact, like the attempt to learn an unknown language without a teacher". Where there is no pressing reason to suspect tradition, historians should no doubt pay careful attention to it: but in this case to build on the assumption that the traditional view is essentially correct is to take for granted one of the very points in dispute. The problem of the character of Richard III is in large measure the problem of the validity of the Tudor traditions about him. Gairdner tried to be just and to base his narrative on documentary evidence: but his attitude is that of a prosecuting counsel rather than of a judge, always inclined to fill gaps in the evidence from Tudor tradition (especially More), and to assign bad motives for possibly creditable acts of Richard, because that tradition asserted him to be a villain. Thus, after admitting that the evidence for Richard murdering Prince Edward at Tewkesbury rests "on very slender testimony and that not strictly contemporary", he nevertheless accepts the traditional view of the matter; and Gloucester's foundation of chantries for his deceased father, brothers, and sisters, shortly after the death of Clarence, is interpreted as a sign of an uneasy conscience instead of being treated as a possibly sincere act of piety.

No more does the Elizabethan tradition of Richard's devouring ambition, fed by numerous crimes from an early age, rest on sure foundations. During the lifetime of Edward IV, Richard seems, in contrast to Clarence and others, to have been conspicuous for his fidelity to his eldest brother. There is, for example, in Polydore Vergil's narrative, hostile to Richard though it was, no suggestion that Richard at that period cherished any designs on the

crown: that suggestion entered the Tudor tradition only
with More's biography. It is More, too, who first hinted
that Richard had a hand in Clarence's death, and even
More is careful to say that this is only rumour. We have
seen that there is no contemporary evidence for Richard's
participation in the death of Edward of Lancaster, and the
same is true of Richard's reputed poisoning of his wife;
even later writers either omit the charge altogether or
report it as a rumour, not a proven fact. Rather stronger,
though still unsatisfactory, is the evidence for Richard's
alleged project to marry his niece. We need not reject the
statement of the usually well-informed and moderate
continuator of the *Croyland Chronicle* that a rumour spread
just before the death of Queen Anne of Richard's intention
to marry Elizabeth in order to thwart Henry Tudor. But
the same writer records Richard's denial of any such
intention, first in Council and later in public; and it would
not have been to the King's interest to contemplate such a
match. His title to the crown would not have been
strengthened by marrying a woman whom the law had
declared a bastard; and to have repealed that declaration
would have been to call into existence her right to the
crown at his own expense. Moreover, if he had thought of
such a marriage, it would not have been a criminal design,
as such a plan would be now. The union of an uncle and a
niece was apparently almost unknown in England and
generally abhorred there: but such marriages had been
legalised by papal dispensations before Richard's time, and
other princes of Latin Christendom were to make use of
this device in later days.

But if this reminder that Richard was a man of the

fifteenth century may work in his favour in this case, it may work against him in some other respects. We have to recall that it was an age of violence and civil war, and that scruples about murder would be unlikely to deter men, brought up in such an atmosphere as Edward IV and his brothers had been, from killing a rival king if it seemed in their interests to do so. Yorkist propaganda asserted that Henry VI died of pure displeasure and melancholy: but an investigation of his remains has indicated that he died a violent death. Moreover, contemporaries specifically mention Richard as implicated in the murder of Henry VI; these sources comprise not only London chroniclers, who might be expected to remember what rumours were current in London, and do not mention Gloucester in connexion with the execution of Clarence, but also include writers such as Warkworth and Comines, who refrain from accusing Richard of any part in the death of Edward of Lancaster.

It is, however, not the death of Henry VI but the disappearance of the Princes in the Tower which has gained for Richard the greatest condemnation—and the most strenuous defence. A thoroughgoing admirer of Richard, such as Sir Clements Markham, had no difficulty in showing the defects of Sir Thomas More's famous account; and if it stood alone, it might leave us unconvinced. But the report that Richard murdered his two nephews is found in a large number of sources, not only in England, but overseas; and it is incredible to ascribe every rumour of such a deed to the malevolence and ubiquity of Bishop Morton and the diabolical cunning of Henry VII. And not only do a number of writers give this report (including a contemporary visitor to London, Dominico Mancini whose narrative has been published since Markham wrote), but there is not so much as a hint in any source that the boys were in fact murdered by Henry VII. Markham would explain this by arguing that Henry VII ruthlessly suppressed all knowledge or even rumours of his crime, which was the more effectively cloaked by spreading the notion that it was Richard III who had done it. But apart from the fact that rumours of the death of the Princes were current before the accession of Henry VII, this view does not fit in with what we know of the efficiency of early Tudor government. Even a modern totalitarian dictatorship finds it hard to keep locked up the skeletons in the cupboard; and in early Tudor England, with its slow communications and its army and police dependent for their working on the co-operation of the middle and upper classes, it was far more difficult to do so. If Henry VII's government was so efficient that it could suppress every report of the Princes being still alive in 1485 and of their subsequent murder, it ought to have been able to produce a clearer and firmer story of their murder by Richard III than we actually have. If the Princes were alive throughout the reign of Richard III, it is very hard to account for their permanent disappearance after the summer of 1483, and for Richard's failure to show them in public to scotch the rumours of their deaths. Moreover, the skeletons of the two boys discovered in the reign of Charles II at the foot of the staircase in the White Tower seem to support the reports of their murder by Richard. In 1933 the urn in Westminster Abbey containing these skeletons was opened, and the bones were medically examined by

Professor W. Wright. In spite of some difficulties in the evidence which he did not discuss, he appears to be correct in his conclusion that the bones were consistent with the sizes and ages of the two Princes in 1483[3]. Besides these considerations it is perhaps of minor consequence that Markham's thesis necessitates a Henry VII as completely villainous as the Shakespearian Richard. Markham supposes, for example, that Elizabeth of York loathed her husband as the murderer of her brothers, and that her mother died in strict imprisonment because she discovered the truth. But there is evidence that Elizabeth of York and Henry VII had a mutual affection, and that he not only granted Elizabeth Wydeville a competence (since her estates had been confiscated by Richard), but made her godmother to Arthur, Prince of Wales, in preference to his own mother, and negotiated for her marriage to the King of Scots at a time when her imprisonment is alleged to have already begun.

If Henry VII is more satisfactorily explained, not as a complete villain, but as a complex character, so is Richard III. He could, as Duke of Gloucester, make himself popular in the North by the better justice and greater order which he promoted in that wild region, so that the York records could lament his death as a great heaviness to the city; and yet he may have been involved in the murder of a defenceless old king. He could be brave, able, and resolute in campaign and battle: but he could be fearful for his own safety and ready to sweep out of his path those

[3] I am not myself competent to evaluate the medical evidence; but R. G. Harrison, Professor of Anatomy in the University of Liverpool, has very kindly read Professor Wright's report and examined the accompanying plates for me.

who seemed to threaten it. He could be honest and patriotic, as in the negotiations at Picquigny, when most of those around him were corrupt: but he could give way to a personal ambition which brought rebellion and civil war to his country once more. Above all, he could usurp the throne, but not because of long-planned villainy.

It is absurd to portray Richard scheming from his teens to gain the crown; for who could have foreseen the death of the splendidly-built Edward IV at the age of forty and the royal minority without which there could have been for Richard no chance of the throne? In fact, he seems to have been outstandingly loyal to his brother Edward, in adversity as well as success. By the late King's will Richard was entrusted with the care of his heir and kingdom; and Gloucester's first acts seem to show that he meant to care for his nephew as faithfully as he had served his father. But the Prince of Wales had hitherto been in the custody of the Queen's kinsmen, the Wydevilles[4] and Greys; and since they knew that, as upstarts, they were intensely disliked by the old nobility, and that the protection of Edward IV was now withdrawn, they tried to control the government through the new King. They sought to exclude the Dukes of Gloucester and Buckingham, the leaders of the blood royal and the old nobility, from every position of influence. This policy alarmed the Dukes, for even if no immediate harm should befall them, the new King would, if allowed to grow up under the tutelage of the Queen's kinsmen, be led to favour their ambitions and share their dislikes. It was less than forty years since the previous Duke of Gloucester, also uncle

[4] [This name is more familiar in its modernised spelling, Woodville.]

of the reigning monarch and also heir presumptive, had (so it was now generally believed) been murdered by the clique surrounding the then King. Equally alarmed by the actions of the Queen's party were those who, like Lord Hastings, had been trusted councillors of Edward IV and now foresaw their exclusion from power. The confidence inspired by Richard's previous reputation and the widespread distrust felt for the Queen's party combined to place him in a strong position when, with Buckingham, he determined to get his blow in first; and so he arrested the King's guardians—Rivers, Grey, and Vaughan—at Stony Stratford on the way to the early coronation which the Wydeville party had planned to end Richard's influence in the government.

Once they were under lock and key, once the Queen had fled to sanctuary, and the rest of her kinsmen had scattered, Lord Hastings' attitude began to change. It did not suit him and others who had been influential in the government of Edward IV that power should go to rivals such as the Duke of Buckingham, the Earl of Northumberland, Lords Howard and Lovell, who had already given particular support to Richard and were now rewarded by him with fees and offices. In resentment Hastings began negotiations with the Wydeville party against this new danger. These rivalries confronted Gloucester with a very unpleasant choice. If he should try to come to terms with the Queen's kindred, it would be hard to be sure of conciliating them, and the young King, after what had happened at Stony Stratford; and an alliance with Hastings and his group, even if it could be achieved, might lose him Buckingham's more valuable aid. After trying in vain to win over Hastings while remaining in league with Buckingham, Gloucester seems to have decided to make sure of his power, and of the further support of Buckingham, Howard, Northumberland, Lovell, and their followers, by striking down Hastings and the Queen's kindred. So Hastings was suddenly arrested in Council at the Tower of London and beheaded without trial the same day (13 June),[5] the Queen was denounced as a conspirator against Richard, and the execution of Rivers, Grey, and Vaughan was decided upon.

This *coup d'état* may have solved Richard's immediate difficulties, but only at the cost of creating greater problems beyond—if he should remain loyal to his nephew; for the remaining members of the Queen's party would now be irreconcilable foes, and the young King might be permanently alienated. Gloucester seems to have been an impulsive man, and he evidently decided to cut the knot by seizing the crown. There may have been some truth in Bishop Stillington's story of Edward IV's pre-contract with Lady Eleanor Butler, and Clarence is said to have already flung against Edward the taunt of bastardy. But there do not seem to be adequate grounds for asserting that Edward IV was illegitimate; and to use a technical

---

[5] On pp. 454-5 of vol. VI (1891) of the *English Historical Review*, Gairdner demolished Markham's contention (made in an article in the same volume) that Hastings was executed, not on the day of his arrest, but a week later after a regular trial; but as Markham nevertheless reasserted the same theory in his book of 1906, and this theory has been repeated since then by Markham's followers, it may be useful to cite a piece of evidence which does not seem to have been hitherto noticed in this connection. *The Inquisitio post mortem*, the usual official enquiry into the estates of a deceased tenant of the Crown, was, of course, made by Richard's own officials; and it stated that Hastings died on 13 June.

RICARDVS · III · ANG · REX ·

Richard III, portrayed by an unknown artist.

Calais in the time of Henry VIII.

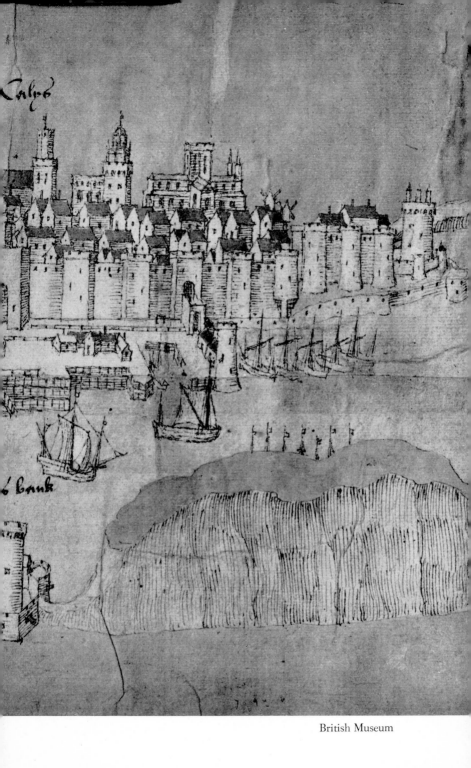

Calys

banke

British Museum

The Great Hall of Berkeley Castle. The Castle was altered
for greater domestic comfort in the late Middle Ages.

impediment to invalidate his marriage was not only unscrupulous but almost bound to weaken the Yorkist
dynasty whose interests Richard had previously so
strenuously defended. The charges were so widely dis-
believed, and Richard's elevation to the throne was
resented by so many of the nobility and gentry, that he
started his reign on a dangerously narrow basis of power.
This led him to shut up the Princes closely in the Tower,
for fear of demonstrations in their favour: but this act
precipitated the very unrest he feared. The widespread
movement in the important South of England, for the
liberation of the Princes, seems to have convinced Richard
that he would not be safe until they were dead; and in his
impulsive way he probably ordered their murder. But
their disappearance increased his troubles instead of
lessening them; and Buckingham, who had helped him to
power, joined the coalition of Queen's kinsmen, displaced
administrators of Edward IV, and Lancastrians which rose
against him.

The suppression of this rising averted the immediate
peril: but the defection of Buckingham and his supporters
reduced still further the unsure foundation of Richard's
power, a basis rendered even more insecure by the death
of his only son in April 1484, and of his wife in March 1485.
He tried hard to live down the past and gain support by
his energy and devotion to his kingly duties. And, in spite
of later denigration, it must be owned that during his
brief reign he displayed many qualities which, if he had
come to the throne in a more acceptable way, might have
helped him to a long and successful reign. He showed zeal
for trade and English interests abroad; he tried to repress

disorder and promote justice; he made it easier for poor
suitors to present their petitions to him and his Council;
he strove to make financial reforms and lessen the burden
of royal demands for money; he instigated a land law (on
uses) which foreshadowed an important reform of Henry
VIII. His public policy in these matters, together with his
tenderness to clerical privileges, his building of churches,
his advocacy of morality among the people, and his
patronage of learning, moved the clergy assembled in
convocation to praise him for his "most noble and blessed
disposition". He endeavoured to win popular approval by
his magnificent dress, his princely building, his care for
heraldry and pageantry, his generous magnanimity
towards the dependents of some of his fallen opponents,
his many recorded acts of kindness to petitioners in dis-
tress. He seems to have met with some success in this
endeavour; and we find the Bishop of St David's writing
to the Prior of Christ Church, Canterbury: "He contents
the people wher he goys best that ever did prince; for
many a poor man that hath suffred wrong many days have
be relevyd and helpyd by hym. . . . God hathe sent hym
to us for the wele of us al". If he could have prolonged his
reign to twenty years instead of two, he might have over-
laid with success and good deeds the memory of his path
to the throne. Had not King John survived the murder of
his nephew and died, many years later, a specially protected
son of the Church? But popular acclamation was a frail
substitute for the support of the aristocracy and gentry,
who had been so largely alienated that the many time-
servers among his remaining adherents doubted his power
to survive. This proved his undoing; for it must be

recognised that what brought him to defeat and death at Bosworth Field was not the feeling of the nation at large, but the desertion of a few great nobles and their forces.

To the Elizabethans his death was the fitting and morally necessary end of a monster, after a whole lifetime of scheming villainy. The modern investigator is more likely to be impressed by the play of events on a complex nature, in an age of contradictions of character. If Edward IV had lived to the age of fifty instead of dying at forty, Richard might have gone down in history as a very commendable character, with a possible share in the murder of Henry VI as the only conspicuous blemish. He might have been remembered as an able and energetic administrator, a brave and skilful soldier, a faithful brother and affectionate father, a kind and generous man of culture, fond of music and architecture, a patron of learning, and a devoted son of the Church. But the responsibilities and perils of an unexpected royal minority aroused in his nature the elements of fear, ambition, and impulsive ruthlessness which led him further and further along the path of immediate expediency at the expense of duty and honour. Even then his will to be a successful and popular king might have enabled his considerable talents to re-establish his reputation, had he been granted time; it is now generally agreed that the portraits of him as King show an anxious and nervous man rather than a cruel or merciless one[6]. But time was not on his side, and he was vouchsafed

---

[6] As for the hunchback, the portraits of Richard do not show any deformity. A contemporary traveller, Nicolas von Poppelau, found Richard's appearance impressive though rather emaciated; but there is some evidence that one shoulder was slightly higher than the other.

only two uneasy years; and, as Bishop Stubbs rightly said, he owes "the general condemnation, with which his life and reign have been visited, to the fact that he left none behind him whose duty or whose care it was to attempt his vindication".

Yet even in Tudor days men sometimes dared to speak good of him, and not only in the North of England. In 1525 Cardinal Wolsey was pressing the Mayor and Aldermen of London for a benevolence. To their objection that this demand was contrary to a statute of Richard III the Cardinal retorted: "I marvell that you speak of Richard the third, which was a usurper and a murtherer of his awne nephewes". The reply to this is noteworthy, and one sentence in it might serve as a partial epitaph on Richard III. "Although he did evill, yet in his tyme wer many good actes made".[7]

[7] [Dr Myers's article gave rise to an instructive correspondence. As he commented, a detailed reply "would have needed a letter nearly as long as the original article". The interested reader must be preferred to those parts of this correspondence published in *History Today*, IV, 1954, 706-10.]

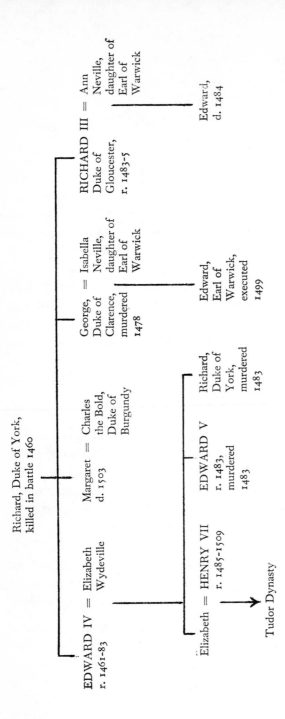

Richard, Duke of York,
killed in battle 1460

EDWARD IV = Elizabeth
r. 1461-83   Wydeville

Margaret = Charles
d. 1503   the Bold,
           Duke of
           Burgundy

George, = Isabella
Duke of   Neville,
Clarence, daughter of
murdered Earl of
1478   Warwick

RICHARD III = Ann
Duke of   Neville,
Gloucester, daughter of
r. 1483-5   Earl of
             Warwick

Elizabeth = HENRY VII
            r. 1485-1509

EDWARD V
r. 1483,
murdered
1483

Richard,
Duke of
York,
murdered
1483

Edward,
Earl of
Warwick,
executed
1499

Edward,
d. 1484

Tudor Dynasty

THE YORKIST KINGS

Dorothy Margaret Stuart

WILLIAM CAXTON
Mercer, Translator, and Master Printer[1]

In the year 1468, when Johannes Guthenberg died at
Mainz, there occurred in the city of Bruges an event that
determined the time and the place of the first introduction
into England of the art with which his name must always
be linked—the art of printing. This event was the marriage
of Edward IV's sister, Margaret of York, and Charles the
Bold, Duke of Burgundy.

To the merchants of London and to their shrewd King,
the political and commercial advantages implicit in the
Anglo-Burgundian alliance were clear: what no one could
then have foreseen was that within the next decade a new
and decisive influence would be thence brought to bear
upon the lives of all but the most abjectly illiterate Englishmen. The young Duchess, coming from a country divided
and to some extent impoverished by the Wars of the
Roses, must have looked with wonder and delight at "the
Florence of Flanders", with its lordly libraries, its skilful
limners, illuminators and architects, its classically-minded

---

[1] [Copyright © Dorothy Margaret Stuart. Originally published in
History Today, x (1960), pp. 256-64.]

pageant-masters. With her, as her "presenter", came a
kinsman of hers by marriage even better qualified than
herself to appreciate these things—Antony, Lord Scales,
later second Earl Rivers, eldest brother of Queen Elizabeth Wydeville; and in the Tournament of the Golden
Tree, held to celebrate her wedding, one of the doughtiest
combatants was Louis de la Gruthuyse, Governor of
Holland, a lavish patron of scholarship and art in Flanders.

Margaret of York must soon have learned that the head
of the English trading fraternity in Bruges, the "Governor
of the English Nation"[2], was a certain William Caxton, who
had served the King, her brother, faithfully and skilfully
in various negotiations, usually but not invariably connected with the wool trade. Born in Kent about the year
of Henry V's death, and speaking English all his days with
the broad accent of his native Weald, Caxton had been
apprenticed in 1438 to an honoured member of the
Mercers' Company, Robert Large by name. A year later
he saw his master's "riding", or mayoral procession, to
Westminster, when sixteen trumpeters attended, blowing
silver trumpets purchased especially for the occasion: but
he was not fated to serve the full seven years of his ap-
prenticeship in Large's house near Old Jewry. The mercer
died in the spring of 1441, and among the many bequests
in his complicated will was one of twenty marks—about
£300 in modern currency—to William Caxton. He may
about that time have arranged for the uncompleted indentures to be transferred to some English, or even
Flemish, merchant in the Low Countries; all we know for

---

[2] A voluntary association of merchants. They dealt in spices and
manuscripts as well as in wool.

certain is that before Caxton had reached his twentieth
year he had quitted England for the dominions of Philip
the Good, Duke of Burgundy, and that he remained overseas, in ever-increasing prosperity, for the best part of
three decades. He was loth, none the less, to sever the last
link binding him to the Mercers' Company, for he returned
to London in 1453 in order to be formally admitted to its
Livery. He did not stay to take part in the "riding" of his
fellow-mercer Geoffrey Fielding in the October of that
year, thereby incurring a fine of three shillings and fourpence. By the date of the Anglo-Burgundian marriage, he
had been for about five years Governor of the English
Nation in Bruges.

Though Caxton declared that he was "bounden to
praye" for the souls of his father and mother, who in his
youth "sette him to scole", whereby he got his living, he
was always diffident, almost apologetic, about his learning.
He could of necessity speak and read French, though
"frensh of Paris" was to him "unknowe". The Flemish
tongue, in which much of his business was transacted, did
not rank as a literary language; some smattering of Latin
he must have had; but he possessed gifts of much greater
worth than wit, eloquence, or mere bookish accomplish-
ment. He had a lively mind, a prehensile intelligence, a love
both of edifying works and "mervayllous historyes", and
a constant desire to win grace for himself in the world to
come by improving the morals and the manners of his
fellow-countrymen here below.

The exact date at which he gave up his Governership
and entered the service of Duchess Margaret is as uncertain
as the motive for the change. It has been suggested that he

wished to marry, and it seems that he acquired both a wife and a daughter some time between 1470 and 1475 : but the seemingly austere rule under which the Governors and their associates were required to live may simply have meant that women would be barred from their official headquarters overseas. It seems more probable that his destiny, in the person of the young Duchess, was beckoning him towards pursuits more rewarding than any connected with commerce or diplomacy.

Only five months before the wedding festivities in Bruges, Caxton had begun to translate into English the French version of the Tale of Troy compiled from various Latin originals by Raoul Le Févre, one of Duke Philip's chaplains[3]; but, conscious of his own, "unperfightness", he had lost heart and laid aside the five or six "quayers" which were all that he had attempted. Yet this lover of "mervayllous historyes" could not forget the *Recueil des Histoires de Troye*, and when the Duchess summoned him to her presence to discuss "divers maters"—he being then in receipt of a "yerly ffee and many other goode and great benefites" from her—he ventured to mention the "quayers" and was promptly commanded to produce them. Catching fire, one imagines, from his obvious "plesyr and delyte" in the *Recueil*, she not only bade him continue the task to the end, but also corrected the "defaute" that she perceived in his English.

It cannot have been with reluctance that he obeyed. After pursuing his labour in Ghent, he completed it in

[3] [Caxton, on his own authority, is generally said to have begun his translation of the *Receuil des Histoires de Troye* in March 1469, after and not before the wedding of Charles of Burgundy and Margaret of York in July 1468.]

Cologne on 19 September, 1471. Affairs, the Duchess's, her brother's, or his own, took him at that season to what he calls that "holy cyte", where it happened that there had been set up one of those new machines known as a "press", upon which was in full swing the novel process of "putting in enprint", namely, printing from movable types instead of stamping crude impressions from rigid wooden blocks.

Caxton had promised "dyverce gentilmen" that he would send them copies of the *Recuyell of the Histories of Troye* in due course; but his pen being worn out, his hand weary and "not stedfast", and his eyes dimmed with "overmoch lokyng on the whit paper", he set himself, at "grete charge and dispense" to master this new art that would enable him to disseminate the fruits of his industry far and wide. From whom he learned the art is not known: but that he learned it at Cologne seems certain. His apprentice, Wynkyn de Worde, will have it so, and Colard Mansion, his future partner, had not then set up the press at which they were working together in Bruges a few years later.

In the meantime, the fortunes of the houses of Lancaster and York had again been reversed in England. In October 1470, King Edward, accompanied by his brother of Gloucester and his brother-in-law, Earl Rivers, had hastily to take ship at King's Lynn on his way to a rather problematical refuge in the domains of the Duke of Burgundy. Whatever the Duke's sentiments may have been on this occasion, Louis de la Gruthuyse, Governor of Holland, felt no hesitation. He received and entertained the fugitives most generously—an action to be remembered with lively gratitude by two of their number, Earl Rivers and the

English King. By the middle of February 1471, Duke Charles had perceived that Edward's chief enemies, Warwick and Clarence, were puppets in the hands of Burgundy's most formidable foe, Louis XI. His support, though given somewhat tardily, was decisive. The three Englishmen, all future patrons of William Caxton, sailed back to their own country; and the spring-time of the year saw the overthrow of the Lancastrians, first at Barnet and then at Tewkesbury.

Four years later the *Recuyell of the Histories of Troye* was issued from the press at Bruges, in folio, without title-page or colophon, its Prologue in red type telling the story of the translation and commending it, and the translator, to the grace of the Duchess Margaret[4]. The type used is Number 1 of the eight used by Caxton in the course of his career. It is said to have been formed upon the handwriting of his partner, Colard Mansion, who had previously worked as a scribe and an illuminator under the patronage of Louis de la Gruthuyse. Not until 1481 were wood-cut illustrations introduced.

In the same year of 1475, the Caxton-Mansion press issued the English partner's translation of "a little French book late come into his hands". This was *The Game and Playe of the Chesse*, written originally in Latin by Jacobus de Cessolis and translated independently of each other by two French clerics. Caxton used both versions, even borrowing from that of 1360 much of a dedication to

[4] [The date and place of printing of many of Caxton's books are matters of controversy. The reader may conveniently consult the list of seventy-one works attributed to Caxton's press at the end of Sir Sydney Lee's article in *The Dictionary of National Biography*, III, London (1908), pp. 1295-8.]

K*—E.S.G.

Prince John of France (the future John II) for the benefit of "the right noble, right excellent vertuous prince, George, Duke of Clarence". For obvious reasons, this dedication was omitted from the second edition that appeared eight years later, embellished with crude wood-cuts.

Duke Charles succeeded in checkmating King Louis XI's pro-Lancastrian machinations in England: but he could not frustrate the King's long-term plan for the disintegra-tion of the duchy of Burgundy, which, being a male fief, reverted to the French Crown after the Duke's death on the battlefield at Nancy in 1477. In the meantime Caxton, perhaps conscious of things to come or perhaps en-couraged by friendly words from King Edward and Earl Rivers, took what must have been a difficult and was certainly a momentous decision. He quitted his Flemish home, and transferred himself and his printing-press to Westminster. There, in a "shopa" hired from the Abbey at a yearly rental of 10s., he set up the first English press. In 1483 he was paying rent for at least four tenements, one of them being over the porch of the Almonry. A note in the handwriting of the Prior tells us that on a particular occasion the rent was paid *in Vino*. The sacrist who made the first entry was John Esteney, afterwards Abbot of Westminster; he is mentioned in the Prologue to one of the last publications of the press, *Eneydos* (1490).

Various reasons have been advanced for the printer's choice of Westminster. If the "William Caxton" buried in St Margaret's in 1478—with two torches and four tapers at a cost of twenty-pence—was his father, and if Brother Richard Caxton, who assumed the Benedictine habit in

1473-4 and died Sacrist of the Abbey in 1504, was his kinsman, family ties may have drawn him thither. The Wool
Staple having been moved to the City of London seven-
teen years earlier, active interest in the wool-trade cannot
have influenced him: but the proximity of the court
would in itself provide a powerful enough inducement. It
was from his printing-press "at the Sign of the Red Pale"
that the first book ever to be printed in England emerged
in 1477. This time he was not even partially responsible
for the translation. *The Dictes and Sayengs of the Philo-
sophres* was translated "out of Frenshe into Englyssh" by
"the noble and puissant Lorde, Antone Earle of[5] Ryvers".

The "puissant Lorde" was already on friendly terms
with the master printer, and when, having borrowed a
copy of the French text from his Squire during a pilgrim-
age to Compostella, he became so entranced that he
resolved to set about translating it, what could be more
natural than that he should send certain "quayers" for
Caxton to "oversee"? The "overseeing" having been
tactfully accomplished, the next step was to put the book
"in enprinte".

They discussed the *Dictes* personally, and Rivers suggested leaving out "dyverce thynges", such as the letters
exchanged between Alexander, Darius, and Aristotle.
Caxton agreed: but when he came to collate the two texts,
the English and the French, he saw that omissions had
been made to which he had not agreed—namely, the un-
gallant *Dictes* of Socrates "touchyng wymen". These he
had the audacity to restore, in a serio-comic epilogue. Was

---

[5] "Of" is an error. As to the name "Rivers", its spelling varies with
typical medieval abandon.

it for love of some particular lady that these passages had
been left out? Or were they absent from the old copy of the
French book?[6] Two further editions of the *Dictes and
Sayengs* appeared, one in 1480-1, about the time when
Duchess Margaret visited her English kinsfolk, and one
towards 1488, when the Queen-Consort of England was
Rivers's niece, Elizabeth of York.

The second production of the Westminster press would
seem to have been Caxton's own translation of *The
History of Jason*. Living in the dominions first of Duke
Philip and then of Duke Charles of Burgundy, the some-
time Governor of the English Nation must have been
made constantly aware of the history of that hero and the
quest of the Golden Fleece. Heraldry, pageantry, courtly
flattery, were all made to do obeisance to the Fleece, which
was the emblem of one of the most illustrious knightly
orders in Europe. Edward IV and his brother-in-law,
Duke Charles, had exchanged compliments in the shape
of their respective orders. Charles was gratified by his
Garter, and Caxton's choice of Jason suggests that the
English King on his side was also well content. Jason was
a topical as well as a courtly choice, and the printer-

6 There had been at least one particular lady in the life of Earl Rivers,
namely Gwentlian, a member of the ancient Anglo-Cymric family of
Stradling, whose founder had acquired St Donat's Castle, by marrying
an heiress, *tempore* Edward I. In 1477 Margaret (by courtesy Wydeville),
his daughter by her, was of marriageable age, indeed may have been
married already to Robert Poyntz of Iron Acton, to whom she bore a
son three years later. That son was christened Anthony. Robert Poyntz
was one of the executors named in the will hastily written by Rivers on
the eve of his execution at Pontefract in 1483. It follows that whatever
sins may have weighed upon the sensitive conscience of this most
likeable of the Wydevilles, neglect of this one sequel of an illicit love
cannot have been among them.

translator tells us proudly that it was under the shadow of the King's noble protection that he had "enterprised taccomplish this sayd litel boke": but of course he would not presume to offer it to His Highness, not doubting that he possessed it in French, "which he wel understandith". He hints adroitly that, with the approval of the Queen, he will present it to his most fair and most redoubted young lord—"oure tocomyng sovereign lorde", the Prince of Wales.

A year later Earl Rivers had another translation "put in enprint", "in feverer the colde sesonn". This time he "Englished" the *Moral Proverbes* of Christine de Pisan: and the ensuing year, 1479, saw the publication of his translation of *Les Quatre Derrenières Choses Advenir* printed (in French) on the press in Bruges on the eve of Caxton's return to England. So eager was the noble translator to see the *Cordyale or the Four Last Things* made accessible to the world of literate Englishmen that the printer felt in duty bound to set to work on the morrow of the day that the manuscript was put in his hands, remembering the "manifolde benefites and large rewardes" he had received.

There is among the Harleian MSS. (B.M. No. 4431) an exceptionally interesting copy of the *Proverbes* of Christine de Pisan. It is believed to have been one of the many rich volumes looted by John, Duke of Bedford, from the French royal library in the Louvre, and it certainly passed into the possession of his second wife, Jacquetta of Luxembourg, whose autograph signature it bears. Jacquetta left all her belongings to the eldest son of her second marriage, Anthony, Earl Rivers. The autograph and motto of "ARIVIERES" appear in capital letters on the same page and beneath them, in black-letter, the autograph and motto of Louis de la Gruthuyse. It may well have been, as Sir Edward Madden conjectured, the actual book used by Rivers when translating the *Proverbs* and a gift from him to his Burgundian friend.

Thus, in an atmosphere of philosophy, medieval mythology and traditional piety, began the procession of books, upwards of a hundred in number, that moved outward from Caxton's press up to the very day of his death in 1491. Of these over a third survive only in fragments or in unique copies. Of seventy-seven recognised (or recognisable) titles, forty-five per cent are devotional, twenty-nine per cent literary or historical, fourteen per cent instructive, and twelve per cent "official", i.e. statutes, indulgences, etc.

Gibbon permitted himself to sneer at Caxton's crude and "unclassical" taste. Did he expect an Aldus on Thames-side, an Elzevir born more than a hundred years before his time? He who, either as translator or as printer, gave to his compatriots in this new, quickly duplicated and disseminated form Chaucer's *Canterbury Tales* and his *Troilus and Cressida*, Gower's *Confessio Amantis*, Lydgate's *Temple of Glass*, Boethius on the *Consolations of Philosophy*, Malory's *Morte d'Arthur* (called by Caxton simply *Kyng Arthur*), Higden's *Polychronicon*, and *The Book of the Knight of the Towre* deserved well of his generation and of ours. Nor were the noble Romans neglected. Cicero, under his middle name of "Tullius", is twice remembered. Who translated *De Senectute* is uncertain; but *De Amicitia* was undoubtedly "reduced in to our englyssh" by that "famous Erle" of Worcester whose head had been lopped off by the Lancastrians eleven years before.

William Caxton loved to hob-nob with his readers, to insert reminiscences, anecdotes and exhortations, to advance beyond the clatter and thump of his press and hold them in easy, intimate converse. Thirty years of exile had not diminished his essential Englishness. In his knack of humorous characterisation he was not so much an imitator as a spiritual son of "that noble, grete philosophre, Geffery Chaucer", though no symbolical eagle ever came in a vision to bear him off to the stratosphere of the Muses. Particularly Chaucerian is the Epilogue to *The Fables of Esope*, which records a dialogue between two priests, of whom one was "quyck and coude putte hymself forth" and the other was "a good symple preest" who might have been a twin-brother of the Poure Persoun of a Toun. There is also a faint Chaucerian echo in the anecdote (in the Prologue of *Eneydos*) of the merchant whose ship was becalmed in the Thames, and who came ashore and went to a house and asked for "eggys": and the "good wyf answerde that she coude speke no frenshe". The merchant was angry, "for he also coude speke no frenshe", and he would have returned eggless to his ship had not a fellow-merchant interposed to ask for "eyren".

The printer who did not hesitate to admonish his readers felt himself sometimes to be admonished by them. In the Prologue quoted above, he confessed that he feared he would not please some gentleman "which late blamed me, sayeing that in my translacyons I had overcuryous termes, and desired me to use olde and homely termes", and he defends himself stoutly, though he stands

"abasshed" between "honest and grete clerkes", that
have clamoured for "the most curyous termes", and other
patrons who would have preferred him to stick to the
"olde and homely". "Certaynly", he admits, "it is harde
to playse every man bycause of dyversite and chaunge of
langage."

William Caxton was indeed a prey to those difficulties
implicit in any period of transition. His span of life was
chequered by many changes and he was fated to see
honoured figures and illustrious friends fading mysteriously or tragically from his sight. Nothing was allowed,
however, to halt or deflect the steady flow of his dedica-
tions. After Edward IV's untimely death and the cruel
elimination of "the gentle Rivers", even when the "most
fair and most redoubted younge lorde", Edward Prince of
Wales, had vanished like a shadow, he felt no compunction
in presenting *The Order of Chivalry* to his "redoubted
naturel and most dradde soverayne lord, kyng Richard".
Has any apologist of Richard III suggested that Caxton
may have had personal knowledge of the fate of his former
patron's eldest son that cleared Richard in the printer's
eyes from any tincture of guilt? Otherwise it is difficult to
understand how he could conclude the Epilogue thus:

> And I shalle pray almyty god for his long lyf, & prosperous
> welfare, that he may have victory of al his enemyes and
> after this short & transitory lyf to have everlastyng lyf in
> heven.

Six books were printed at the sign of the Red Pale
during the brief reign of the last Plantagenet, but under the
Tudors royal patronage was not lacking, to Caxton himself up to the time of his death, and thereafter to his

successor, Wynkyn de Worde. The old printer's al-
legiance could be transferred without much difficulty
when there was no heir-male of the ancient dynasty in the
field. Lady Margaret Beaufort, the bookish mother of the
first Tudor, commanded him to translate the romance of
Blanchardyn and Eglantine, and his translation duly
appeared in 1489, with a Prologue apologising for his
"rude and comyn englysshe". In his pleasure at being
openly patronised by the Tudor Court, did he banish
utterly from his recollection another royal Margaret, his
first patroness, the first corrector of his "defaute", not far
away in Malines, unreconciled to the new dynasty and
eager to plot against it when occasion should offer? She
certainly would have been ill pleased if she could have seen
the dedication of the *Eneydos* to her former servant's "hye
born . . . tocomynge naturell & soverayn lord Arthur, by
the grace of God Prynce of Walys, Duc of Cornewayll,
Erle of Chester". Yet here was a second "tocomynge
soverayn" who never came to the throne.

During the last years of Caxton's long career, 1490-91,
almost all the books issued from his press were of a devotional tinge. We encounter no more chatty or courtly,
discursive or edifying Prologues and Epilogues; the only
Epilogue, though interesting historically, is brief and
comparatively colourless. It is appended to *The Fifteen Oes*,
a collection of prayers each of which begins with the
vocative O, and it runs:

> "Thiese prayers tofore wreton ben enprinted bi the
> commandementes of the moste hye & vertuous pryncesse
> our liege ladi Elizabeth, by the grace of god Quene of
> Englande & of Fraunce, & also of the right hye & most

noble pryncesse Margarete Moder unto our soverayn lorde the kyng."

The only known copy is a quarto in the British Museum (MS. Harl. 2255), and it is bound up with several tracts printed by Wynkyn de Worde. The elaborate wood-cuts, especially the very fine full-page crucifixion, suggest that efforts have been made to render the little book worthy of the two royal ladies who had wished that it should be "enprinted".

Curiously enough, that unmartial prince, Henry VII, desired Caxton to translate and "enprinte" *The Fayttes of Armes*, a sort of manual likely to be of service to every "gentylman and man of werre". The Epilogue, with its fulsome flattery of Henry VII, would have displeased Margaret even more than the Prologue of *Eneydos*.

Wynkyn de Worde published the *Lyves of the Fathers* upon which Caxton was working in 1491, and which he "fynyshed at the laste daye of hys lyff". If the earliest and greatest of English printers had been granted more fulness of days, the last work to come from his press might well have been of an entertaining rather than of a devotional nature. In the British Museum, Egerton MS. 1982, this tantalising scrap is preserved:

> On a leaf of paper pasted on the inside of the ancient cover of this MS. (Mandeville) and too friable and decayed to be separated from it there was written—
> "Thys fayre Boke I have fro the Abbey of Saint Albons in thys yeare of our Lord M.CCCC.LXXXX the sixte daye of Apryll.
>
> > Willyam Caxton."

Nine years later Wynkyn de Worde gave the travels of

Sir John Mandeville to a delighted and unsceptical world.

It was in St Margaret's and not in the Abbey that Caxton was buried. 7s. 8d. was paid for torches at his requiem and 6d. for the tolling of the bell, but neither tomb nor tombstone has survived to mark the grave.

Considering that illustrations printed from wood-blocks had been used in conjunction with letterpress printed from movable metal type, some time before Caxton's first press was set up, it seems curious that he should have shown so little enterprise in this regard. According to William Blades (*The Biography and Typo-*

Sean Jennett: *Pioneers in Printing*
(Routledge & Kegan Paul)

Woodcut of chess players, one a king the other a clerk, from the illustrated second edition of Caxton's translation of *The Game and Playe of the Chesse.*

graphy of William Caxton) only fifteen of the known books
printed by him are thus illustrated. In the earlier examples,
such as the second edition of *The Game and Playe of the
Chesse*, the pictures are quaintly crude, nor does the artist
seem invariably to have been mindful of the text. The
nine-and-twenty Canterbury pilgrims have dwindled to
twenty-four and it is difficult to determine who the lady
in a *hennin* can be, unless upon the hypothesis that the
same block had already been used for another supper-
table scene. On the other hand, some of the devotional
works near the end of the printer's long life contain some
items of real and poignant beauty. Such are the Crucifixion
in *The Fifteen Oes*, and the *Image of Pity* to which an
indulgence was attached for the soul's weal of all those
who "pyteously beholdyng" the Image should devoutly
say five *Paternosters*, five *Aves* and a *Credo*.

SELECT BIBLIOGRAPHY

1. GENERAL OUTLINES OF ENGLISH HISTORY IN THE
FIFTEENTH CENTURY

DENTON, W. *England in the Fifteenth Century*. London (G. Bell & Sons) 1888.

GREEN, V. H. H. *The Later Plantagenets: A Survey of English History between 1307 and 1485*. London (Edward Arnold) 1955.

HOLMES, G. *The Later Middle Ages, 1272-1485*. Edinburgh (Nelson & Sons) 1962. Vol. II of A History of England, edd. C. Brooke and D. Mack Smith.

JACOB, E. F. *The Fifteenth Century, 1399-1485*. Oxford (Clarendon Press) 1961.

KINGSFORD, C. L. *Prejudice and Promise in Fifteenth Century England*. Oxford (Clarendon Press) 1925. Repr. London (Frank Cass) 1962.

MCFARLANE, K. B. "England & the Lancastrian Kings, 1399-1461", in *The Cambridge Medieval History*, Vol. VIII. Cambridge (University Press) 1936. Provides a useful summary.

MYERS, A. R. *England in the Later Middle Ages*. 2nd revised edn. Harmondsworth (Penguin) 1963. Vol. IV of The Pelican History of England. Covers the period from 1307 to *c*. 1526.

WILLIAMS, C. H. "England: The Yorkist Kings, 1461-85" in *The Cambridge Medieval History*, Vol. VIII. Cambridge (University Press) 1936. Provides a useful summary.

2. THE WARS OF THE ROSES

CHRIMES, S. B. *Lancastrians, Yorkists, and Henry VII*. London (Macmillan) 1964.

LANDER, J. R. *The Wars of the Roses*. History in the Making. London (Secker & Warburg) 1965. Mainly original sources.

MCFARLANE, K. B. "The Wars of the Roses", in *Proceedings of the British Academy*, L (1964). Offers an authoritative interpretation.

3. SOCIAL AND ECONOMIC HISTORY

BARTLETT, J. N. "The Expansion and Decline of York in the Later Middle Ages", in *Economic History Review*, 2nd series, XII (1959-60).

BEAN, J. M. W. *The Estates of the Percy Family, 1416-1537*. Oxford Historical Series. London (Oxford University Press) 1958.

— "Plague, Population, and Economic Decline in the Later Middle Ages", in *Economic History Review*, 2nd series, XV (1962-3). Considers a basic problem of the period.

BENNETT, H. S. *Six Medieval Men and Women*. Cambridge (University Press) 1955.

— *The Pastons and Their England: Studies in an Age of Transition*. Cambridge Studies in Medieval Life and Thought. Cambridge (University Press) 1932.

BRIDBURY, A. R. *Economic Growth: England in the Later Middle Ages*. London (Allen & Unwin) 1962. The conclusions are controversial.

CARUS-WILSON, E. M. *Medieval Merchant Venturers*. London (Methuen) 1954.

COLEMAN, O. "Trade and Prosperity in the Fifteenth Century: Some Aspects of the Trade of Southampton", in *Economic History Review*, 2nd series, XVI (1963-4).

Du BOULAY, F. R. H. "A Rentier Economy in the Late Middle Ages", in *Economic History Review*, 2nd series, XVI (1963-4).

DUNHAM, W. H. Jr. "Lord Hastings' Indentured Retainers, 1461-83" in *Transactions of the Conneticut Academy of Arts and Sciences*, XXXIX, New Haven, Conn. (1955), and separately New Haven, Conn. (Yale University Press) 1955.

GREEN, A. S. *Town Life in the Fifteenth Century*, 2 vols., London (Macmillan) 1894. Still the most complete description of the subject.

HARNETT, C. *The Wool Pack*. London (Methuen) 1951, Puffin Books, Harmondsworth (Penguin) 1961. A children's novel that is authentic and detailed.

HAY, D. "The Division of the Spoils of War in Fourteenth Century England", in *Transactions of the Royal Historical Society*, 5th series, IV (1954).

HOLMES, G. A. *The Estates of the Higher Nobility in Fourteenth Century England*. Cambridge Studies in Economic History. Cambridge (University Press) 1957. Still relevant for the fifteenth century.

LEWIS, N. B. "Organisation of Indentured Retinues in Fourteenth Century England", in *Transactions of the Royal Historical Society*, 4th series, XXVI (1944).

JEFFS, R. "The Percy-Poynings Dispute", in *Bulletin of the Institute of Historical Research*, XXXVI (1961).

McFARLANE, K. B. "Bastard Feudalism", in *Bulletin of the Institute of Historical Research*, XX (1943-5).
— "Parliament and Bastard Feudalism", in *Transactions of the Royal Historical Society*, 4th series, XXVI (1944).
— "The Investment of Sir John Fastolf's Profits of War", in *Transactions of the Royal Historical Society*, 5th series, VII (1957).
— "England in the Hundred Years War", in *Past and Present*, 22 (1962).
— "A Business Partnership in War and Administration, 1421-1445", in *English Historical Review*, LXXVIII (1963).

POSTAN, M. M. "The Fifteenth Century", in *Economic History Review*, IX (1938-9).

POWER, E. *The Wool Trade in Medieval English History*. London (Oxford University Press) 1941. Basic material in the concluding chapters.
— *Medieval People*. London (Methuen) 1924, Pelican Books, Harmondsworth (Penguin) 1937. Sketches of Thomas Betson and Thomas Paycocke.

POWER, E. and POSTAN, M. *Studies in English Trade in the Fifteenth Century*. London (Routledge and Sons) 1933.

PUGH, T. B. and ROSS, C. D. "The English Baronage and the Income Tax of 1436", in *Bulletin of the Institute of Historical Research*, XXVI (1953).

4. FIFTEENTH CENTURY GOVERNMENT

BALDWIN, J. F. *The King's Council*. Oxford (Clarendon Press) 1913.

CHRIMES, S. B. *English Constitutional Ideas in the Fifteenth Century*. Cambridge (University Press) 1936. Reveals the underlying concepts of the time.

FORTESCUE, Sir JOHN *The Governance of England*, ed. C. Plummer. Oxford (Clarendon Press) 1885. Repr. London (Oxford University Press) 1926. A contemporary view of fifteenth century government.
De Laudibus Legum Anglie, ed. and tr. S. B. Chrimes. Cambridge Studies in English Legal History. Cambridge (University Press) 1949.

FRYDE, E. B. and M. M. "Public Credit, with Special Reference to North-Western Europe: England", Chap. VII pt. IV of *The Cambridge Economic History of Europe*, III Economic Organisation and Policies in the Middle Ages, edd. M. M. Postan, E. E. Rich, E. Miller. Cambridge (University Press) 1963.

HARRIS, G. L. and WILLIAMS, P. "A Revolution in Tudor History", in *Past and Present*, 25 (1963).

HASTINGS, M. *The Court of Common Pleas in the Fifteenth Century.* Ithaca, N.Y. (Cornell University Press) 1947.

LANDER, J. R. "The Yorkist Council and Administration, 1461 to 1485", in *English Historical Review*, LXXIII (1958).
— "Council, Administration, and Councillors, 1461 to 1485", in *Bulletin of the Institute of Historical Research*, XXXII (1959).

ROSKELL, J. S. *The Commons in the Parliament of 1422.* Manchester (University Press) 1954.
— *The Commons and their Speakers in English Parliaments, 1376-1523.* Manchester (University Press) 1965.

Select Documents of English Constitutional History, 1307-1485, ed. S. B. Chrimes and A. L. Brown. London (A. & C. Black) 1961. The materials are mainly in English after 1422.

WILKINSON, B. *Constitutional History of the Fifteenth Century, 1399-1485.* London (Longmans) 1964. A recent survey with translated documents.

WOLFFE, B. P. "The Management of English Royal Estates under the Yorkist Kings", in *English Historical Review*, LXXI (1956).
— "Henry VII's Land Revenues and Chamber Finance", in *English Historical Review*, LXXIX (1964).

5. ANTI-CLERICALISM AND HERESY

DICKENS, A. G. *Lollards and Protestants in the Diocese of York, 1509-1558.* London (Oxford University Press for the University of Hull) 1959.
— "Heresy and the Origins of English Protestantism", in *Britain and the Netherlands*, II edd. J. S. Bromley and E. H. Kossman. London (Chatto & Windus) 1964. A convenient summary.

McFARLANE, K. B. *John Wycliffe and the Beginnings of English Nonconformity.* Teach Yourself History Library. London (English Universities Press) 1952.

OWST, G. R. *Preaching in Medieval England. An Introduction to Sermon Manuscripts of the Period c. 1350-1450.* Cambridge Studies in Medieval Life and Thought. Cambridge (University Press) 1926.

— *Literature and Pulpit in Medieval England.* Rev. edn. Oxford (Blackwell) 1961.

THOMPSON, J. A. F. *The Later Lollards, 1414-1520.* Oxford Historical Series. London (Oxford University Press) 1965.

6. ENGLISH ART, LITERATURE, PRINTING,
AND ARCHITECTURE

AURNER, N. S. *Caxton, Mirrour of Fifteenth Century Letters.* London (Allan & Co.) 1926. Repr. New York (Russell & Russell) 1965.

BENNETT, H. S. *Chaucer and the Fifteenth Century.* Rev. edn. Oxford (Clarendon Press) 1958.

BLADES, W. *The Biography and Typography of William Caxton.* Rev. edn. London (Trübner) 1882.

CHAMBERS, E. K. *English Literature at the Close of the Middle Ages.* Rev. edn. Oxford (Clarendon Press) 1947.

EVANS, J. *English Art, 1307-1461.* Oxford (Clarendon Press) 1949.

The History of the King's Works, ed. H. M. Colvin, I-II, London (H.M.S.O.) 1963.

PEVSNER, N. *The Buildings of England.* Harmondsworth (Penguin) since 1951.

THOMPSON, A. H. "The English House", in *Social Life in Early England; Historical Association Essays,* ed. G. Barraclough. London (Routledge & Kegan Paul) 1960.

TURNOR, R. *The Smaller English House, 1500-1939.* London (Batsford) 1952. Illustrations to early chapters.

WOOD, M. *The English Medieval House.* London (Phoenix House) 1965.

7. EUROPEAN BACKGROUND

HEERS, J. *L'Occident aux XIVe et XVe Siècles: Aspects Économiques et Sociaux.* Paris (Presses Universitaires de France) 1963.

WALEY, D. *Later Medieval Europe.* London (Longmans) 1964.